PUBLICATIONS OF THE TEXAS FOLKLORE SOCIETY
NUMBER XXXI

MODY C. BOATRIGHT, Editor
WILSON M. HUDSON, Associate Editor
ALLEN MAXWELL, Associate Editor

The Golden Log

PUBLISHED BY
SOUTHERN METHODIST UNIVERSITY PRESS
DALLAS

The
Golden Log

EDITED BY

MODY C. BOATRIGHT
WILSON M. HUDSON
ALLEN MAXWELL

SOUTHERN METHODIST UNIVERSITY PRESS: DALLAS, TEXAS

LIBRARY OF CONGRESS CATALOG CARD NUMBER: 61-17184

PRINTED IN THE UNITED STATES OF AMERICA
BY WILKINSON PRINTING COMPANY: DALLAS, TEXAS

Contents

The Golden Log

The Golden Log:
An East Texas Paradise Lost

FRANCIS E. ABERNETHY

I FIRST HEARD the following East Texas story, with its Paradise Lost theme (A1331), ten years ago from a student of mine at Woodville, Texas, High School. She told it with only the scantiest of detail, and I do not remember whether she accepted it as fact or as fantasy. More recently Walter Lavine of Ruliff, Texas, told me a variant of the story; this time the setting was across the river in Louisiana. I have been passing this tale on for several years, every time I discussed the sources of *Paradise Lost*. In comparison with the first version I heard, current versions have grown; but this has been a growth in detail, not a change in essence.

There used to be a place where the sawmill and the commissary were on one side of a big, deep creek and the settlement on the other. But the people never had any trouble getting across because there was a big golden log spanning the creek and it was easy to walk across.

Since this was the only crossing for many miles either way, the mill boss and everybody really kept an eye on this golden log to keep anything from happening to it, and there was a general understanding that the log was to walk on and nothing else. But the women got to chipping off a little every once in a while and trading it in to the commissary agent for new clothes and bedspreads and things like that.

Everybody in the settlement was doing real well and they didn't need the money, but that's the way they were.

Well, they chipped and whittled on the sly and the log got smaller and smaller, but they cut it down so slowly that nobody ever noticed it. There were a few more people than usual falling in the creek, but still nobody thought much about it—except the women, of course; they knew.

Finally one day a new bride came across, going over to get some flour and a new enamel water dipper. She got to the middle of the log, looked all around, but didn't see anybody, so she bent over and chinked herself out a piece of gold and said to herself, "I believe I'll get me a new dress to look pretty in for the dance next Saturday night." She walked a little farther and said to herself, "It won't hurt to have some new shoes to go with it"; and she looked all around and then cut another little chunk out. She got across the log, stopped, and thought, "Takes a new hat to really get started in." One more look and she stepped back to the log, leaned out a little, and sliced a long sliver right off the top.

That last sliver was all it took. The log cracked and popped real loud and sank right to the bottom of the deepest hole in the creek. The mill boss heard the noise and came running down from the office. He caught her standing there and she had to tell what she had done, so he told her and her husband to pack up and leave the settlement. He took the commissary agent to the county seat and had him thrown in jail.

After that nothing seemed to go right at the mill. Every time the creek rose nobody came to work. They tried to build a bridge but it washed out every time there was a heavy dew. Finally it got so bad that the mill had to shut down and everybody left.

Nobody can tell you where that place is now. Some say it's in the Thicket; others say it's in Louisiana. But they all agree that a man could sit in a rocking chair on his front porch and shoot a deer any afternoon and that they baited their trotlines with five-pound bass. It must have been some place!

This story is fairly typical of tales which an older generation romantically spins about the good old days when the forests were filled with game, the rivers were teeming with fish, and living was easier, happier, and less complicated. It was thus in Eden when Adam and Eve, the sun grown round that very day, had dominion over the fish and fowl and every living thing that moved upon the earth. The setting is an East Texas paradise which furnishes all things that are necessary for life; it is an idealization of a secure rural existence.

The new bride and her husband are our Adam and Eve. This time, Adam is entirely out of the action of the story and is mentioned only as he leaves. As in the biblical tale, the woman becomes the culprit and is guilty of the crime that brings about their expulsion. Unlike the story as told in Genesis, here the man has no hand in the immediate business; but we can safely assume that he is guilty through knowledge of the deed and by association, as was Adam. Both Eve and her East Texas counterpart were unable to withstand a temptation to advance themselves. Eve succumbed to a desire for knowledge and equality with the gods, while our bride lusted after material riches and a desire to elevate herself sartorially to the level of the bosses' wives. In both cases, ambition and a thirst after worldliness lost the world for all concerned in the story. Sir James Frazer in *Folk-Lore in the Old Testament* discusses the fall of man in the various mythologies, but does not consider any, except the Hebraic, which emphasize the wickedness of the human being as we see it in Eve and the young bride.

The commissary agent plays the devil in our story. In most mythologies man loses his paradise and finds death because he is misled by a messenger from God or is duped by an evil one who has intercepted a message from God. In

Genesis, Satan as the serpent leads Eve to the luxury of the tree of knowledge instead of the necessity of the tree of life; in our story the crooked commissary agent offers material luxuries instead of the simple necessities of life. The main difference between the two tempters is motivation. Biblically the tempter is personified Evil, whose motivation, very vaguely presented, seems to be a mischievous desire to cause trouble. We know even less about the commissary agent than we do about the biblical serpent. Our only conclusion is that he was ambitious for wealth. There is no evidence that he was trying to cause dissension among the mill hands or that he was antagonistic toward the mill boss, as Milton's Satan was toward God.

The mill boss can easily be equated with God. This is not difficult when one recognizes the mill boss's authority in a sawmill community. He hires and fires; pays off, gives credit, and collects; arbitrates disputes; and is the supreme power from whom all blessings flow. In this case he settles the problem with speed and decisiveness, and poetic justice is rendered to all major participants. The same swift and immediate justice is found in the biblical version: "Therefore the Lord God sent him forth from the Garden of Eden, to till the ground from whence he was taken."

The central symbol in the community is the log, considered in the telling as a part of a tree. The tree is used universally as a symbol of life and fertility, and here the log—golden, to emphasize its intrinsic value to the community, and typical in its central position of sacred trees in Germanic and Celtic folklore—insures the prosperity and the continuing livelihood of the community. Frazer, in *The Golden Bough*, points out that the tree-of-life concept is made more specific among certain primitives, the Maoris for instance, when they fabricate tales in which trees become the umbilical cords of mythical ancestors, connecting the present generation to their parent stock and to an other-worldly Paradise. The East Texas golden log is also a silver cord, an *umbilicus* which links the children of the settlement to their material sustenance, the sawmill and the commissary. When the log is finally cut in two, the people are separated from their sustenance, maternal in its way, life in paradise is lost, and they are forced to leave their idyll to make their livings elsewhere—and their sorrow is greatly multiplied. As Roark Bradford concludes his tale, "Eve and That Snake": "So de Lawd bailed ol Adam's trover and leveled on his crop and mule, and put Adam and Eve off'n de place. And de next news any yared of old Adam, he was down on de levee tryin' to git a job at six bits a day."

Thirteen Tales from Houston County

THEODORE B. BRUNNER

THE AREA from which these tales were gathered lies in an exclusively agricultural and lumbering region in the Piney Woods of East Texas. The eastern section of Houston County was comparatively prosperous at the turn of the century. At that time the largest sawmill in the South was located near the present community of Ratcliff.

Farming went into a decline in this region when prohibition appeared on the national scene. Many of the residents turned to the less laborious and more profitable occupation of moon-shining, the heavy forest cover providing excellent protection for still sites. The repeal of prohibition, coinciding with the Great Depression, brought ruin to many of the small farmers in the area. Much of the surrounding land was purchased by the federal government and now forms the Davy Crockett National Forest.

Completely enclosed by the national forest, the small farm communities of Kennard, Ratcliff, and Hagerville exist much the same as during the middle of the last century. The Rural Electrification Administration provided power lines to the area only ten years ago. Many of the original pioneer dwellings, some heated solely by large open fireplaces, are still occupied. Television reception has been possible only within the past three years. No telephone service is available for farm homes.

The inhabitants of the area are almost exclusively of old British stock, although a few Negroes descended from slaves

8

brought into the region before the War Between the States are also to be found. Virtually no immigration into the area has occurred during the past fifty years.

The area is unusually homogeneous in many other respects. No extremes of wealth or education are present. There exists among the people of the area a strong sense of their origin in the pioneer era. It is hardly possible for a newcomer to be completely accepted into the community, though overt hostility toward strangers is not shown. Farmers cheerfully extract mired automobiles from the unpaved, winding country lanes without thought of monetary reward. This homogeneity produces the type of community in which local mores take precedence over formal, written law. Few Anglo-Saxon settlements in Texas come closer to the conventional concept of the folk community.

Radio and television have almost taken over now, but only a generation ago the telling of tales and the singing of ballads were the primary sources of entertainment for child and adult alike in rural East Texas. The adult tales were first to vanish; the children's tales, preserved by old grandmothers, endured longer. A scene that was common in the East Texas of thirty years ago on long winter evenings consisted of the old grandmother seated in front of the open fireplace surrounded by her grandchildren. Perhaps one child would massage the old woman's legs and a second would rub the back of her neck and pretend to search for lice amid the white strands of hair. All would listen with rapt attention as the old lady unfolded one tale after another without pause.

Thirteen tales are set down here in the approximate language of the tellers. At the head of each is a brief comment in which the informant is identified and motifs and tale types are discussed.

Hard Times

The teller of this tale was Mrs. Euphratus Rainbolt, whose maiden name was Euphratus Steed. She was born in Houston County on Novem-

ber 27, 1915, and had a high school education. She heard this and the
two following tales before she was of school age, some forty years ago.
This story is allied to tale types 1541, 1650, and 1653. The prominent
motifs are K362.1, a numbskull who has been told to keep his sausage
"for the long winter" loses the sausage to a thief who calls himself Long
Winter; K359.2, a thief beguiles the guardian of goods by using an
equivocal name; K1413, a numbskull who has been told to "guard the
door" does so literally by wrenching if off and carrying it around with
him; and K335.1.1.1, a door falls on robbers from a tree and scares them
into abandoning their loot.

Once there was an old man and lady that lived all by
themselves out in the woods, and they didn't have any neighbors
and nothing to do. The old man went off ever'day to work and
told the old lady to stay there and mind the door. At night he'd
come home and bring his money and hide it up in the loft and he
just had sacks of money hid up there, and the word got around.

There was a lot of robbers in those forests at that time, and
one of 'em hid near his house and heard him tell his wife when
he come home one day that he was saving that money for
hard times. And she says, "My, he must need a lot."

So one morning when the old man left, he told her to mind
the door. And so he hadn't been gone long when the robber
come up to the gate and hollered, "Hello!" And she said, "Who
are you?" And he said, "I'm Hard Times." She said, "Lawd!
Come in. My husband has been saving money for you for
years." She crawled up in the loft of the house and tossed
it all down to him.

That night she met her husband as he came in the door,
and she said, "Old man, you can't guess what happened today."
He said, "No." "Well, Hard Times come and I give him all
that money you been saving for him."

Well, he just turned around and walked out of the house
without sayin' a word, and she took after him. When she
went out the door, she pulled it to, and it come off the hinges,
and she just drug it along with her. They walked until night.
Come to an old stoopin' tree and the old man walked up that

tree to stay all night so the wild animals wouldn't get him, and the old woman followed him right on up the tree, draggin' the door.

They stayed up there and went to noddin' and went to sleep. And in the meantime, this robber that had come and got their money met his feller gamblers underneath this tree. And they were gamblin' and the old woman was noddin' back and forth and nodded too far and dropped the door right in the middle of 'em, and this just scared 'em to death, and they run off.

Well, that woke the old man up and they crawled down out of the tree and gathered up their money, and it was their sacks and their money, and they carried it home, and he explained to her all about hard times, and she never made such a mistake again.

My Mama Cooked Me and My Daddy Eat Me

This, another of Euphratus Rainbolt's tales, coincides rather closely with the Grimms' story known as "The Juniper Tree" (type 720). The chief motifs are the cruel stepmother (S31), relative's flesh eaten unwittingly (G61), murdered child reincarnated as bird (E613.0.1), and bird resumes original form of murdered girl (E696.1). In Grimm the murdered child's bones were buried under a juniper tree so that the father would not recognize human bones. Here only the toenails and fingernails are buried under the apple tree. In both tales the remnants of the child's body are transformed into a bird. In the dungeon scene of Faust Gretchen sings the little bird's telltale song.

There was a man and his wife and several children lived 'way out in the woods and the mother died. Later the man decided that they needed a mother, so he remarried. Now this woman he married was mean to the children, but the father didn't know it. He went off to work ever'day and he didn't know what went on at home.

Of course, they didn't have a lot to eat and the mother wouldn't let the children eat when the father eat—she cooked him meat. This particular day she didn't have any meat to cook for him, so she killed one of the children and cooked it and cut off its toenails and fingernails and made the other children bury 'em under the apple tree and told 'em that if their father asked where the child was to tell him that it had gone to visit its grandmother. So of course, when the father come in that night and had this delicious meat and asked where the other child was, they said that it had gone to visit the grandmother.

The next morning a little bird came up on the rooftop and says, "Come out, old woman, and I'll give you a bag of gold. Come out, old woman, and I'll give you a bag of gold. My mama cooked me, my daddy eat me, and my little brothers and sisters buried my fingernails and toenails under the apple tree. Come out, old woman, and I'll give you a bag of gold."

But the old woman was afraid to come out, and the third morning the little bird came and called to her, the old greedy stepmother couldn't stand it any longer. She came out, and the little bird dropped a big stone on her and killed her.

So the little bird flew down off of the rooftop and was the little girl again and all the children danced around and sang and when the father come home from work, they told him what had happened, and they all lived happily ever after.

I Want My Big Toe

This tale of Euphratus Rainbolt's involves knowing cannibalism. It is type 366. The principal motif is E235.4, return from dead to punish theft of part of corpse. For a study of this tale type see Wilson M. Hudson, "I Want My Golden Arm," in Folk Travelers *("Publications of the Texas Folklore Society," XXV [1953]), pp. 183-94.*

Once there was an old man and woman, and they were very poor, and they didn't have any children. They lived all alone. And the old man died. Now, the old woman didn't want to just completely part with the old man so before she buried him, she cut off his big toe.

Well, it rocked on for a few days and she got hungry. She

decided to put on a pot of turnip greens to boil. And since she didn't have any boiling meat to put in 'em, she decided she might as well just go ahead and put the ole big toe in it. So, she started the turnip greens to cooking with the big toe in it, and it caused the old man's ghost to turn over in the grave.

So that night, she heard the old man's voice: "I want my big toooe. I want my big toooe."

She says, "Where're ya at?"

"I'm in the graaave. I want my big tooooe."

Well, it just scared her to death, but she went to sleep after a while, and the next day ever'thing was all right. But the next night when she went to sleep, she began to hear the old man's voice again, and this time it sounded closer. He says, "I want my big tooooe. I want my big tooooe."

She says, "Where're ya at?"

"I'm on the roooad."

Well, she didn't sleep any more *that* night. But the next day, ever'thing was all right. When she went to bed that night, she was getting dozy, and she heard this voice, "I want my big tooooe. I want my big tooooe!"

And it sounded much closer, and she said, "Where're ya at?"

"I'm in your roooom."

"What! You're in my room?"

"Yeeeees, *I'magonnaget'cha!*"

The Robbers' Gold

This and the next three tales were told by Floyd O'Pry, who was born in Limestone County in 1887 and moved to Houston County in 1915. He had an elementary school education. He is a Baptist minister. This story is notable for its adherence to dramatic form throughout; note that it is made up of conversation only. It begins with a slight motif of inhospitality (W158), passes on to a fear test (staying in a haunted house, H1411), and ends with robbers frightened from their stolen goods (K335.1) Like Mrs. Rainbolt's "Hard Times," it contains a door; but it is not actually the falling of the door that frightens the robbers in O'Pry's story—it is the slipping and rattling of the chain securing the door in the tree.

Knock, knock. *[Sound effect produced by tapping pocket-knife against arm of chair.]*

"Hello. Uh, say, Mister, could we get to stay all night here?"

"No, we haven't got room."

"We're awful tired. Would like to stay all night."

"Well, on down the road about half a mile is an old outhouse. You can stay there if you're not afraid."

"Oh, we're not afraid of anything!"

"Yes, but there's ghosts comes there ever'night."

"We ain't afraid of ghosts."

"Well, you go down this road about half a mile. Out on the right is a big house, is a mansion, built by wealthy folks. They was ever'one killed, and nobody can't stay there at night because of the ghosts that comes."

"Mike, let's go and try it."

"Okay, Pat."

"Well, this does look like a spooky place. I'll tell you what we'll do. We can manage that. We'll get this ol' doah and take them chains there and tie the door up in them two trees there with the limbs close together."

"All right."

"Well, we've just about got it fixed. Listen, Mike, did you hear that?"

"Uh-uh."

"Look yonder! There's a buncha men coming. They got a big sack fulla something."

"They're pouring it out on the floor. Hmmm! Look at the money them fellers is got!"

"Hold it, Mike! My chain is slipping. *[Sound of slipping chain made by rattling knife on the side of chair.]* Watch them men run! They think it's a ghost after them. Hmmm,

mmm! Come on. We'll get that money and hide out fum heah! Mike, we don't have to walk any more. We can ride the train. Whoo-Whooo!"

I Want My Two Big Toes

This is Floyd O'Pry's story. It is similar to "I Want My Big Toe" above, and the notes given there are applicable here. Cannibalism does not seem to be involved in O'Pry's story, since the toes that were eaten belong to a bear; but the bear behaves like a revenant who comes back to punish the theft of a part of his corpse. The questions and answers of O'Pry's story are like those between Little Red Ridinghood and the wolf. For a version very similar to O'Pry's, see Bertha McKee Dobie, "Tales and Rhymes of a Texas Household," in Texas and Southwestern Lore *("Publications of the Texas Folklore Society," VI [1927]), pp. 41-42.*

One time they wuz two little boys walkin' along through the woods where they wuz some traps set, and a big black bear had got caught in one of th' traps and pinched off two of its big toes. So the boys taken th' two toes home and went to th' fireplace and roasted them toes. One of them eat one of them, and the other eat the other.

So they went on ta bed, an' after awhile, somethin' commenced, "I want my two big toooes. I want my two big toooes."

Th' ol' man said ta his wife, "Go 'round there and see what that is sayin' 'I want my two big toes,' wife." So she went out and she couldn't find nothin'. Come back in and it started up again. "I want my two big tooooes. I want my two big tooooes."

So th' feller's wife says, "John, you go out there and see if you can find what that is wantin' its two big toes."

And he went. Looked all around th' house. Looked all around th' fence corners, looked under th' house. Couldn't find a thing and went back in th' house.

And it started up again. "I want my two big tooooes. I want my two big tooooes." So they walked to the chimney and looked up, and there it wuz in th' chimney, a big ol' black bear sayin', "I want my two big toooes. I want my two big toooes!"

And the man, when he looked up, said, "What's them two big eyes there for?"

"To look you through."

"What's them big claws there for?"

"To dig yo' grave."

"What have ya got them big teeth there for?"

"To chomp yo' bones!"

The Master's Homecoming

This story of O'Pry's, like his first one above, is made up altogether of dialogue. The progress from inconsequential news to more and more serious news, connected in a chain, conforms to an ancient pattern known as the climax of horrors (motif Z46, tale type 2040).

"Say Mose, how has ever'thing been gettin' along since I left?"

"All right, Massa, all except one thing. Your ol' coon dog, he died."

"My ol' coon dog!"

"Yassuh, he died."

"How come him ta die?"

"Well, they say it 'uz fum eatin' too much hossflesh."

"Too much horseflesh!"

"Yowsuh."

"How'd he get so much horseflesh?"

"Well, ya see, your barn burned. But that's all. That's all. Just your barn burned and all your stock burned up."

"All my stock burned up and th' barn!"

"Uh, yassuh, but that's all."

"Well, how come the barn ta catch a-fire?"

"Massa, really it caught fum de house."

"What! From the house!"

"Yassuh, ya house burned down."

"What! My house burned down!"

"Yassuh, but that's all. That's all that happened since you been gone."

"Well, how come my house to catch a-fire?"

"Well, Massa, they said it was from the candles that was burnin' that night. But that's all, Boss."

"How come th' candles wuz burnin'?"

"Well ya see, Massa, your mother-in-law died, and dey wuz a-burnin' th' candles, and the house caught fum da candles, and de barn caught fum da house, and da house and da barn burned up, and burned your stock up, and your ol' coon dog got too much hossflesh."

"Well, how come my mother-in-law ta die? What wuz th' matter with her?"

"Well, dey say it wuz fum da shock. But that's all. That's all."

"What shock?"

"Well, dey say that your wife run away wit da chauffeur, and it wuz th' shock that caused your mother-in-law ta die."

Dividin' th' Dead

This last tale of O'Pry's is well known throughout the Old South. Its type is 1791 and its principal motif X424. In a comparative study Miss Hazel Harrod finds the "germ story in a Latin tale dated A.D. 593." See her article, "A Tale of Two Thieves," in The Sky Is My Tipi *("Publications of the Texas Folklore Society," XXII [1949]), pp. 207-14. In a fine Texas version from around La Vernia, the thieves are dividing roasting ears in a cemetery; see Richard Smith, "Richard's Tales," in* Folk Travelers *("Publications of the Texas Folklore Society," XXV [1953]), pp. 245-47.*

Along in slavery times there wuz a ole nigger that had been off to one of the neighbors and wuz comin' in by a cemetery, and he saw some fellas there. They had really been out and stole some peaches, and was dividin' 'em, and had dropped two at th' gate.

The nigger went on home and run in and told his ol' massa that th' devil and th' Lord was down there dividin' th' dead.

He told him, "There's no such a thing as that a-goin' on."

He says, "Yessuh! I saw 'em. One would say you take this one and I'll take that one."

The old man had been helpless for a good while with rheumatism and couldn't walk. So, he told ol' Mose ta take him on his back and carry him down there and he would see fer hisself, and that if it wadn't so, he would get a whippin'.

He says, "All right, Massa, you will see that it is *so*."

So Mose taken his master on his back, carried him down to th' cemetery, walked up ta th' gate, an' shore 'nough out a short ways they could hear 'em sayin', "You take this one and I'll take that one. You take this one and I'll take that one."

Finally, when they finished up what they had with them, they says, "There's two at th' gate. I'll take one and you take th' other."

So the old nigger dropped his boss and hit for th' house. And the old man beat his servant home.

Is He Fat or Lean?

This is Mrs. Washie Lenderman's story. She was born in Houston County in 1887, and had an elementary school education. Her story is historically the same as O'Pry's "Dividin' th' Dead." The question, "Is he fat or lean?" and its answer are found in a fifteenth-century English translation of Étienne de Besançon's Alphabetum Narrationum; *see Harrod, as cited above.*

One time, there wuz two fellers goin' ta steal some sheep. They wanted ta steal 'em a fat sheep ta eat. And they wuz ta meet at th' graveyard when they got their sheep.

So they wuz a ole man had been sick a long time, and he live with his boy. And it 'uz hot weather, and the ole man wanted ta go home. Th' boy told him, he'd take him after supper.

So after supper, he put th' ole man on his back and had started ta take him home. He couldn't walk—hadn't walked in years.

They went by the graveyard, and there wuz a feller stepped out and says, "Oh, you back a'ready. Is he fat or lean?"

And he says, "Fat or lean, damn him, you can have him." And he just throwed him down and went ta runnin', and th' ole man jumped up and beat th' boy home.

Aunt Dutch Sally and the Mean Boys

Mrs. Washie Lenderman is the teller of the three tales about Aunt Dutch Sally, whose real name was Sallie Luce. Aunt Sally, who was thought of as a witch, employed sympathetic magic to avenge herself on the boys who mistreated her (D2063.1.1).

Now this is a real, true story, and I saw the ole lady 'long when I was a little girl. She wuz a old, old lady and she had ta take ma'phine. She'd have weak spells, and if she didn't get her ma'phine, she'd get down and couldn't walk and she might die.

So she wuz goin' a little trail through to a neighbor's house and there wuz two mean boys come along and took her ma'phine away from her. Then they taken her money, what she had in her pocket. Then they whipped her and told her if she 'uz a witch, now to do some a her work.

She broke a little bush and place it down in the road and says, "By the time that bush wilts, you'll be wilted just like it."

And so the bush kin'ly begin to wilt in a few minutes. The leaves turned over. And so they just wilted down right in front of her. They couldn't get up and she just ha-haed, and laughed, and went in their pockets and got her money and her ma'phine, picked up her stick and walked on th' little trail ta th' house and told th' folks about it.

Aunt Dutch Sally and the Feisty Girl

In this story Aunt Sally again employs sympathetic magic for revenge. The motif of stealing a vegetable from a witch's garden is found in the Grimms' story of Rapunzel (G279.2).

One time there wuz a ole lady lived by herself and she wuz
a witch. And so ever'body wuz nice to her. There wuz a
feisty girl come along, and th' ole lady wuz in her garden
fixin' up her plants. She had set out some cabbage, and this
girl just reached down and pulled up one of her cabbages.

And she told her, "Give me that cabbage." And so the
girl threw it at her. She picked it up and broke a leaf off of it
and throwed it down and says, "Now, young lady, you'll wilt
down just like that cabbage for pulling it up."

And so she did. She just wilted down and died. But before
she died though, she was told, "And ever cow that yore daddy
has got will walk around the lot 'til they die, one by one. Until
they ever'one die." And so they did. They walked around in
the lot until they ever'one fell dead.

Aunt Dutch Sally and the Robber

Perhaps Aunt Sally's big cat is evidence that she is a witch. Capture
by blinding is a recognized motif (K783).

One time there wuz a ole lady and she wasn't afraid a
nothin'. She lived by herself. She just had a little ole log
cabin and she had it chinked all around with rags and mud,
and her ole fireplace wuz a whole end a th' house. She'd just
drag in logs as big as she could drag and put 'em in th' fire
and just let th' ends of 'em stick out. As they would burn,
she'd push 'em on up in the fire.

She had a little money along and she told fortunes, and
they wuz always somebody there, but that night there wadn't
anybody there, and a big ole robber come. There was a big
hole in the back of the chimbly, a great big hole. You could
see through it. She saw this robber's eyes. She had a big ole
cat, and it lay on the hearth. She fussed at th' ole cat, and
it lay on the hearth. She had a big shovel there and lots of
hot fire, jest red coals and ashes. She fussed at th' cat two or
three times and says, "If you don't get up from there and

get off of that hearth, I'm a gonna throw some ashes on ye."

That just tickled th' ole robber, and he wuz looking through ta see her throw th' ashes on th' cat, and she just picked up th' shovel and got her a good shovel of red fire and coals and just sent it through that hole and put his eyes out.

He couldn't see, and she went ta hollerin' fer help. They come and they got 'im. So she got through.

That's Once

Mrs. Dona Sue Curry, who was born in Houston County in 1923 and went through high school, told this story. It is allied to the taming-the-shrew type; a special motif number, T251.2.3, has been assigned to the situation in which a "wife becomes obedient on seeing husband slay a recalcitrant horse." This motif is found in Italian and Spanish tradition. Mrs. Curry's version has a touch of subtlety in that it does not explicitly point out the wife's immediate reform. A version from West Texas adds that the wife was good and obedient ever afterward. In this version a newly married rancher has hitched a mule to his buggy and the mule balks. See Stanley W. Harris, "Stories of Ranch People," in Singers and Storytellers ("Publications of the Texas Folklore Society," XXX [1961]), p. 175.

There was this very prominent farmer finally decided that he was goin' to take him a wife. Every woman in the community thought that he would be the catch. So he finally decided on one.

He went to the church that day to his wedding and he rode the most beautiful white stallion you ever saw. He really was crazy about this horse. In fact he had told his wife how much he loved this horse, how much it meant to him and ever'thing. So he took his wife after they were married and he put her on the back of this horse and started home.

They had gone down the road about a mile or so, and the horse stumbled. He said, "Well, that's once."

They went on a little bit further, three or four miles, and the horse stumbled again. He said, "Well, that's twice."

And just as they were riding into the barnyard, the horse stumbled again, and he jumped off and just shot it dead.

And his new bride jumped all over him. She fussed and she hollered at him. She couldn't imagine why he would want to do a thing like that.

And when she was all finished, he said, "Now, that's once."

The New Telephone Wire

This story was told by Mrs. M. G. Wonmuck, who was christened Georgia Anne Mahalie Landcaster in Trinity County in 1895. The motif of the bumpkin who thinks that articles can literally be sent by telegraph (J1935) is found in America.

Saturday at dinner they loaded on a bale of cotton and this old man carried it to the gin. Come back and told his wife, "They're a-puttin' in the outfit that I never heard of in my life."

"Well," she says, "husband, what wuz it?"

"Well," he says, "they call it a telephone wire. I never saw nothin' like it."

"Ooh! I do wish that I could go see it."

"Well," he says, "kindle up, work hard, and if we get out another bale of cotton by next Saturday at dinner, we'll load it on, and I'll carry you up there to see the telephone wire."

Well, she decided that they wasn't gonna quite make it and she hired two children to come and help 'em so they would get out th' bale a cotton by Saturday night.

Well, they got there. They got there with the bale of cotton. And she hurried up and walked along under the wire. It was about a mile long then. She'd hold her hand over her eyes and look and watch.

"Well," he says, "now have you saw the telephone wire?"

She says, "Yeah, I saw it. I'm ready to go."

He says, "Old woman, what do ya thinka that?"

"Well, old man, I think it might be all right to send papers and letters on, but when they put a bale a cotton up there, POP she'll go."

So there you see, people been green as I am, always.

Homemade Tales

RICHARD M. RIVERS

The Tellers

"BACK IN THOSE DAYS provisions, food, was scarce includin' salt. People had to raise what they eat on the farm. There was no grocery stores but what was grown on the farm there. Now in the fall of the year why there would be say a half a dozen men in the settlement, and they would hitch up the mule wagons and drive down to a salt lake. They called it Lake Bristonow, down about seventy-five miles south of where I was raised. A pair of mules would walk down there in about three days. They'd take the big black washpots; they'd hold ten maybe fifteen gallons of water; and they'd go down there and boil that salty water until it would make salt. It wouldn't be fine. It would be coarse salt. They'd have to beat it up to salt the meat with when they went back home. That would be in the fall of the year before the hog killin' time come around.

"On rainy days when the farmers—farmers worked from early mornin' til night in those days. There were no hours to quit and start on. They worked by the sun. And so rainy days there was say three or four or half a dozen of these men get together, sorta like they did in the salt business, and they'd go down and take the stand down in the woods where the deers run. Deers have a run. And another man would take a half a dozen old hound dogs and go way off back half a mile or more away and get them old hounds started in behind a bunch of deer. They'd come down by these men. They had

23

the old double-barrel cap shotguns loaded, and as the deer run by they'd shoot down maybe two or three, as many as they needed. They wasn't killin' them for sport. They was killin' them for meat. So they'd take the deer and dress them, and they'd have deer meat to eat."

As the old man talked, he rocked way back in the large old rocker. Satisfaction met the tired corners of his mouth and smoothed the little clefts. It was a satisfaction of remembering the things that pleased him most, things long past, things which he thought no one could possibly have been interested in but himself. He was happy that someone was interested. His words came slowly and deliberately. Yet there was an anxiousness in his speech as if he could not get it all out. "Times was hard in those days," he would say. "We had to raise potatoes of both kinds and peas. We had to thrash the peas out, so when the winter came we'd have something to eat." Despite the hardness of the times, the old man told of them with gusto, remembering only the adventure of having lived through them.

Church Thomas was born in 1876 in a small settlement in North Louisiana called Blackburn. So small was it, that there was no doctor to deliver the boy. As a child, Church lived two miles away in a small farmhouse of hand-dressed plank. His boyhood was spent much as any child growing up in a frontier settlement in the 1820's would have spent his, for while that area was not by any means on the frontier, it was so remote that existence there was pioneer-like. Food was grown, meat was hunted, and wheat-flour bread was still a very rare thing.

Church's formal education was slight. He took short courses in arithmetic and geography and barely managed to get through the fourth reader. Most of his time was spent with the cotton, which was their money crop. After it was picked and crudely baled, Sogum and Mandy were hitched up for the long drive into the inland port city of Shreveport. This was Church's only touch with civilization, and it was on these long drives that the tales which are recorded here were "swapped" between his father, his older son, and the few Negroes that accompanied them.

Like Church, his wife Eloise was born on a small farm—in Cass County, Texas, in 1890. She began her "schoolin'" early, but it was constantly interrupted by the cotton picking or the potato harvesting. As a result, her formal education consisted of only nine years at a small country school. While the farm was fairly remote and could only be reached by a blazed trail through the pines, there was, nevertheless, a relatively large town of two thousand people nearby. This provided the unheard-of luxuries of grocery stores and even a dress shop, and evidences of these fragments of civilization can be found in her tales.

The third storyteller is different from the first two. Her tale is definitely part of a long-standing oral tradition passed down from mother to daughter for a period of four generations. Unlike Mr. Thomas' "swaps" and Mrs. Thomas' "scary tales," Mrs. Maude Foster's tale has a traceable history. Having moved from Seneca, South Carolina, her grandmother brought this "homemade tale" as a bedtime story.

While growing up in a remote and densely wooded section of Marion County, Texas, Mrs. Foster was ten miles from the nearest small settlement. She was taught by her grandmother and then sent "into town" to go to school. Ten years of public school made up her formal education. Despite this, her tale retains an almost primitive flavor of the early frontier.

All of the following tales except one have been transcribed from tape.

The Tales

DON'T FORGET THE BEST
Church Thomas

Well, once upon a time they was a young friend of a very rich man visited him, and he had a beautiful cave of everything imaginable on earth in this cave. And the young man was so thrilled with the thoughts of just being in there with this rich friend, that he was thrilled to death. And the rich friend told him, now says, "If you don't forget the best," says, "you can have everything in this cave. Everything is yours."

So they went through and he admired everything so much. He was thrilled to death. And the rich man said to him, again now says, "Everything in here will be yours if you don't forget the best."

And they still went on in throughout the place, and the young man was thrilled to death. And they finally come on out towards the front and everything, and this rich man says now, "This is everything is yours, if you don't forget the best."

Finally they went to the door and walked on out on the outside, and rich man says, "Now," he says, "you forgot the best." And the door had locked to, and he says, "That was the key."

JOHNNY IN THE MORNIN'
Church Thomas

There was a time that best that I can remember that they was a boy and a girl that was very much in love, and the boy was named Johnny. And he wasn't particular about gettin' married at that certain time, but he told his sweetheart, "If you go up on top of this house"—it was a cold night—"and spend the night up there, I'll marry you in the mornin'."

So she went up on top of the house, and 'twas cold, and she was up there just a, "O-ooooooh, I'm gonna marry Johnny in the mornin'." And she's a, "O-ooooooh, I'm gonna marry Johnny in the mornin'." And the last words she said was, "O-ooooooh, I'm gonna marry Johnny in the mornin'." She froze to death.

THE BUNDLE OF STICKS
Church Thomas

Well, best as I can remember is that this story is true. It

was told to me back in the time when I was boy and was about some famous king or president.

This story might be valuable to some of our young men this day and time. There was a famous man once that had three sons, and he was givin' them his ideas about how to start out in life. So he handed his sons a bundle of sticks and he ask them to break them.

Well the first one tried, and the second, and the third he— they all failed. Then the man took the sticks and unbundled them and took the string from around them and took one at the time and broke the sticks. He did this in order to prove to his sons that not to try to do the big things first but learn how to manage the little things as you go up in life. Not start at the top of the ladder and come down but start at the bottom and go up.

THIS LONESOME NIGHT
Eloise Thomas

Once upon a time there lived a little family way out in some dark woods, a man and a woman, and they had a little girl that they called Mary. One day her parents had to go to town to get some food for their family and left little Mary there at home all alone. She waited all day long for them to return, and finally night came on. She was very very lonesome, so she wondered what to do, and she decided to go into the yard and call to someone.

So she says, "Who's going to stay with me this lonesome night?" And she listened and heard a voice way down in the woods answer, "I-I-I- am."

Mary felt better then and ran back into the house to wait, but soon she became very anxious and went back into the yard and called again, "Who's going to stay with me this lonesome night?" The voice answered but was much nearer, "I am."

Again she ran back into the house and closed the door.

She waited and still no one came, and she decided to try to call again. This time she opened the door, and there stood just outside a great big wolf. And he says, "I'm going to eat you all up."

This frightened little Mary very, very much, and she rushed into the house and closed the door quickly. The old wolf was very angry, and it was a very, very cold night, so he ran around the house and kept running, trying to get in. He was very hungry, and he was getting very weak, so he fell to the ground exhausted and froze to death just as Mary's parents came in.

THE DEVIL'S TREASURE
Eloise Thomas

Once upon a time[1] there lived an Indian boy who was called Johnny Bear's Son. He lived with his father and mother in the woods, and he told this story to me. He said that his father had given his soul to the devil, and he had signed a paper saying he would agree to be taken to hell when he died. For this the devil was supposed to show him where a great chest of gold was hidden.

So one night Johnny's father got him out of bed and told him and his brother, "Come with me." They got up and dressed and took a lantern and a shovel and a black book and went outside. The night was very, very dark and cold, and there was no moon or stars in the sky.

They went into the woods and at last came to a little hill. The father told the boys to hold the lantern and not to run away no matter what, and then he began to read from the black book. This book was the devil's book, and he kept saying strange words. All at once the lantern was blown out, and two tiny specks of light appeared and began to dance all about. As they danced they got bigger and bigger, and the old man fell down on the ground like he was dead. Then the balls of fire stopped and stood over one spot. The boys were very, very frightened and began to run and ran home and locked the door.

The next morning they came out to the hill with their mother and all that was left was a boot sticking up out of the ground where he had been drug down to hell by the devil. The mother said this was because the father did not have the courage to look the devil in the face or he would have shown him the treasure.

A HOMEMADE TALE
Maude Foster

Once upon a time a long, long time ago there weren't many houses, and people lived in the country. So there was a family that had a big farm, and the daughter married and moved about three miles away. So in a year or two she wanted to visit her mother, so she took the baby and went across a blazed-out trail that they had blazed out with a hatchet or something to find the way, a nearer way through to her father's farm.

So when she got started she heard something coming up behind her, and it frightened her. She looked, and it was a big bear, and he was gaining on her just getting closer and closer. So she pulled off her shawl and threw it down, and he stopped and tore that all to pieces. That let her rest a few minutes.

She went ahead then and ran. She was tired. She was giving out. So she looked back and the bear was coming again right after her. And then she pulled off the baby's little shoe and threw it down. He stopped and tore that all up.

She ran on. She looked back, and he was still chasing her. He was coming after her, so she pulled the baby's sock off and threw that down and ran again. And she was getting very, very tired.

She looked around and he was nearly catching her again. She ran and ran and ran, and she pulled the baby's other little shoe off and threw that down. He stopped and tore that up.

Then she went on and she came to the fence around the farm, big old rail fence. She climbed over, and he nearly got her at this fence. She ran and called her father, and he heard her. She told him there was a bear chasing her, and he ran in the house and got the gun and met her and killed the bear. So she reached home just fine.

Comments

These tales were all collected from persons living in the small East Texas city of Jefferson. All the tellers were brought up on farms, as I have shown, and at least two of them spent their childhood in rather remote areas of the pine forests. Their way of life, while not quite of a pioneer nature, was by no means an easy one. Most of their food had to be grown and their meat was either raised or supplied by hunting. Their farmland was in a thickly wooded, hilly area, and the fields had to be carved out of the forest. Homes were built of hand-hewn boards and put together with square iron nails. As a result of this upbringing, their tales are full of bears and wolves, blazed trails, ghostly lights, and far-distant voices in the forest. Even the jests speak in terms of caves and cold nights.

Mr. Thomas' tales are actually two jests and an anecdote. "Don't Forget the Best" is a variant of the Open Sesame Type (T676). The supernatural power, that is, the knowledge of the words "open sesame" to gain exit from the treasure cave, has been reversed, however, and now becomes a sort of riddle, "don't forget the best." The story is a little moral tale of greed and ends jestingly when the poor friend becomes so "thrilled to death" that he forgets the means of ever gaining entrance to the cave again. Thus he is not locked in with his treasure, unable to remember the magic words, but he is locked out and cannot obtain "the best." The tale, while basically the same open sesame story of not remembering something, whether magic words or a key, has undergone a transition.

There is a Jamaican variant collected by Walter Jekyll in which a blackbird shows the spider a house full of meat owned by a rather negligent butcher. In order to gain entrance one had to say, "One-two-three me no touch liver." Once inside, of course, the greedy spider takes the liver, which is considered choice, "the best," and cannot get out. While this variant has not changed much from the archetype, it is interesting to note the idea of "the best" is employed.[2]

The story of "Johnny in the Mornin'" is a fragment. Mr. Thomas said that it was originally a longer tale and was told to him by an old Negro woman named Clarice. To appreciate its charm, the tale should be heard. When it is told, the low teeth-chattering moan of the shivering girl and the coarse frontier humor in the last line provide a flavor that is otherwise missed. Nevertheless, it loses none of its delightful wittiness with the delivery of the punch line.

The tale is a jest based on the motif of the humiliated or baffled lover (K1210). It is somewhat like the old fabliaux of Vergil, the wise fool, who calls to his mistress from the street. She tells him to get in a basket that she will lower, and she will pull him up to her window. He does so and is left hanging halfway there to spend a most miserable night.

"The Bundle of Sticks" is a perfect example of a tale that has completely changed meaning through repeated tellings. Fundamentally, it is the anecdote of the quarreling sons and the bundle of twigs (J1021). The archetype is of a peasant who calls his sons to him and gives them a bundle of twigs to break. Of course, they cannot do it until he shows them how. Unbundling the sheaf, he breaks the twigs one by one, illustrating that in unity there is strength. Mr. Thomas' tale contains all these details with the substitution of a king for a peasant, but somewhere in its retelling the original moral has been lost. Now instead of a peasant teaching strength in unity, we have a king teaching humility and forethought.

Both of Mrs. Thomas' tales follow the same pattern of construction. They are neither tale types nor a merging of tale types but are comprised of a series of whole folktale motifs. The tale of "The Devil's Treasure" begins with the motif of the man who sells his soul to the devil (M211). Perhaps the most interesting feature of this tale, however, is the treasure-seeking sequence. This is a linking of two motifs. First, the light indicates hidden treasure (N532). Usually a mysterious light appears to guide one to the treasure. Evidently here the lights are transformations of the devil. The old man will not look at them, thus breaking a taboo which is in effect while the treasure is being indicated (N553). Here, too, we find the idea of looking the devil in the eye to gain power over him, a variant of the old "speak of the devil and he shall appear" belief.

The story ends with a variation of the Lenore of the dead rider motif (E215) when the old man is pulled down into hell. The story motif is also very close to that of the Don Juan tales. Interesting to note is the boot left sticking out of the ground. This is a rather rare motif but can be found in the Coyote cycle with Coyote's wanting to be buried with his head left sticking above ground.

"This Lonesome Night" has the same characteristic structure of linked motifs. The first part of the story has overtones of the children abandoned or the Hansel and Gretel motif (S301)—that is, a little girl left all alone to the mercy of the forest. I mentioned earlier that Mrs. Thomas was the only teller who lived close to any kind of town; notice that in her tale the parents leave to "go to town to get some food." Surprisingly enough, however, her stories are more primitive in tone than any of the others. A sense of the half-real and the mystic hovers over them.

The wolf in this tale is a werewolf (D113.1.1). I am not at all sure that the teller realized this when she told the story, but notice, for instance, that the little girl asks, "Who's going to stay with me this lonesome night?" When she calls the third time and peeps out, the wolf promises to "eat her all up," which is no answer to her question; here it seems that the Little Red Riding Hood story begins to take over.

"A Homemade Story" is based on one of the most common motifs in folklore, the obstacle flight (D672). It has been expanded in order to make a tale, and in this case it has an atmosphere one would expect to find in a frontier story. The blazed-out trail and the old rail fence give it time and place. Notice the extreme reality of the tale in contrast with the older and more supernatural versions of the chase. The pursuing ogre or witch becomes a bear. The comb, the mirror, and the pebble become various pieces of clothing. As I have already pointed out, a very realistic ending is added to make the motif a story. J. Frank Dobie has collected versions much like this tale.[3] In his version a pioneer woman is pursued by a panther and must discard pieces of her own clothing to deter the animal.

Pioneer tales of this sort have a remote similarity to the myth of the descent of the goddess Ishtar (F85). In her journey into the lower world, she must pass a series of sentries or guards, each of whom demands of her a garment. She arrives completely unveiled but obtains all of her clothing on the return journey. In both the bear and panther stories and in "This Lonesome Night" the parents return home or arrive just in time to save the child. This seems to be a common motif among frontier tales.

1. This tale is not transcribed from tape. The teller is my grandmother, and, being very well acquainted with her speech mannerisms, I have retold the tale, keeping as close as possible to the original.

2. Walter Jekyll, *Jamaican Song and Story* (London, 1907), p. 23.

3. J. Frank Dobie, *Tales of Old-Time Texas* (Boston, 1955), pp. 181-94.

Joe Sap, Wit and Storyteller

A. L. BENNETT

JOE SAPPINGTON, in his late years, was a dignified, well-dressed, and affable newspaperman who made visits to our crossroads general store at fairly regular intervals. He was always a welcome guest, as he had been in his youth, for besides being an amiable gentleman he was an excellent spinner of yarns and a salty commentator on the current scene. In order to eke out a slender income as a writer of feature stories syndicated in weekly Texas newspapers, he sometimes sold mutual insurance. But he was a writer by profession, and a teller of tales by natural predilection.

Around the turn of the century no man (except Hogg and Clark, William Jennings Bryan, and Tom Campbell) had impressed his personality on the sturdy citizens of Bell, McLennan, and Coryell counties more than "Joe Sap," as he was known professionally. There must still be hundreds of dusty attics in Central Texas that hold his book—*Joe Sap's Tales (By Himself)*—for this book of tales and commentaries went into a tenth printing (it was published by the Embree Printing Company of Belton, Texas, 1908). It was advertised in the newspapers as "the most laughable book ever published . . . a smile in every line, a laugh in every sentence." This was conscious exaggeration, of course, but the book is occasionally hilarious, and all of it is still good reading. For the social historian, it is a rich source.

Joe Sap was at his best when he wrote of "old times," but

sometimes in his commentaries on the contemporary scene a flash of Sappington wit reminds you of Mark Twain. In his essay on bald heads he remarks, "The Bible says that the hairs of our heads are numbered, which goes to show that head hair has always been a scarce article." Of politics he says, "It has about the same effect on a man that turpentine has on a dog." (The social historian notes that in 1908 turpentining a dog probably did not meet with group disapproval.) "I looked in the dictionary," he continues, "for a definition of politics and found that it is a system of principles of government; then I went to a political meeting and found that Mr. Webster is the biggest liar that ever lived. There is no system, nor principles, nor government about it." On party regularity, however, he only half ironically declares, "I am going to remain loyal to our glorious old party as long as there is a plank left of it big enough to get a toe-hold on. I will stand by it if it gets down to but one lone plank, and that plank declares unequivocally for the free and unlimited coinage of scrap iron."

Sometimes Joe Sap turned the irony on full force. In a delightful sketch called "The Yankee Haters," which comes close to the mood and manner of *Tom Sawyer*, he recounts,

In less than three weeks from the time father had so abruptly reconciled me to the United States government, I had organized a secret society that I named the "Yankee Haters," with headquarters in the loft of Sid Morgan's barn. The object of this organization was to whip and kill Yankees, protect the weak and helpless, fight Indians, hang niggers and otherwise promote the interest and welfare of the country in general.

As I said, Joe Sap was at his best when telling a tale of old times. In Central Texas the event that stirred almost as much excitement as the Confederate Reunion was the old-time "school exhibition" held at the log schoolhouse at the close of the year's educational activities. These exhibitions, or "concerts," were sometimes preceded by dinner-on-the-ground and afternoon baseball games; and the night program included almost interminable recitations, orations, tableaux, and dramatic sketches. People came from miles around and swamped the seating and standing capacity early. The rest milled around outside or peeped between the logs where the "dobbing" had fallen out. Joe Sap's story goes as follows:

One night at a concert in which I was taking the role of the noble lover in some great drama, I had more humiliating mishaps to occur to me at the climax of that play than ever happened to any actor that ever came before the footlights. My execution had just been ordered by the King, on account of some rebellious act of mine against his Majesty's government and I was led out on the stage in front of the four tallow candles that served as footlights, by the King's soldiers, who were armed with muzzle loading rifles, shotguns and old cap and ball six shooters. I folded my arms on my heroic breast and repeated those patriotic words, to-wit: "I die that Rome may live," just like I had been repeating at our rehearsals. The captain cried out to the king's soldiers, "Present arms; take aim; one, two —" and then according to script and our rehearsals, the King's daughter, who weighed at least sixty pounds more than I did, and who was madly in love with me, rushed upon the stage waving a piece of paper and shrieked, "A reprieve! A reprieve!" and fell in a swoon upon my gallant bosom. Everything up to that time had come strictly up to contract; Bill Jenkins had cut loose on "Cotton Eye Joe" and all that was necessary to bring the play to a triumphant close was to pull the curtain. But that curtain wouldn't pull, notwithstanding the fact that Tom French, our property man, was tugging at it with all his might. The curtain failing to move painfully prolonged my contact with the King's daughter, who remained swooning upon my chest, waiting for the wagon sheet that we were using for a curtain to be pulled. To add to my embarrassment, while Tom was tugging at the curtain some fellows in the audience and especially the bunch of hoodlums on the outside, who were witnessing the performance through cracks, yelled all sorts of embarrassing things at me, such as: "Stay with her, little Sap," "I'm bettin' on little Joe," "Brace up there, little Joey," "Hurrah for Sapsucker." And while that bunch of ill bred thugs were yelling at me, Bill Jenkins' fiddle bridge fell with a resounding whack and almost at the same instant, Andy Peters' (one of the King's soldiers) musket went off and shot a right of way through the gable end of the house. Just what happened immediately after Andy's gun went off, or what became of the King's daughter, I never knew. The last thing I saw on the stage that night was Tom French, who, just as the gun fired, broke the curtain rope and fell on his back across the footlights.

I remember Joe Sappington best when he was a young man, a sort of farmer, and came on his mule every Friday night, during one season, to sit on my Grandma Dunne's front gallery and tell stories of the day and of older times. He was too peripatetic and wide-ranging to be a good farmer, but the summer I spent with Uncle Bill and Grandma Dunne (she was a devout Catholic in a sea of Protestantism), Joe Sap was doing all the work on his father's hardscrabble holding. His father had been sick for a long time and the only food that really appealed to him was Grandma Dunne's fresh-baked lightbread.

Friday was Grandma's fast day, but also her day to do the baking for the following week. So on Friday evenings while Joe Sap waited to take a fresh, warm pone of lightbread home to his father, he fell into the storytelling vein. I sat in the doorway hating for feet-washing time to come and listening with utmost respect and attention.

One night he brought us news that Carl Henderson's little three-year-old boy was attacked by an old yellow dog and the child's face was lacerated by the dog's teeth. Henderson's bulldog defended the boy from further harm, but it was learned that the yellow dog had been bitten by a striped pole-cat, the kind that was supposed to carry hydrophobia. Both dogs were kept tied up; since the yellow dog would not eat, it was plain that something was wrong. So the child was taken immediately to Grandma Williams, who was owner of a madstone. The stone was applied to the wounds and for four days and nights the stone adhered to the child's lacerated face, a sign that it was sucking the poison out. The last Joe Sap had heard the wounds were healing rapidly and the child was believed out of danger.

Uncle Bill said, "Grandma Beck, over near Killeen, has been owner of a madstone for years. Quinus Hill went to her not long ago for a mad-dog bite and he's doing all right, the last news we had."

Then Joe Sap, after appropriate transitions, got into his tale of Gray Bess, the old faithful horse that could trail Indians. It went somewhat as follows:

One fall afternoon in the last century, Will Hampton and some of his neighbors who lived near Pearl (Coryell County) were out in Mr. Hampton's pasture looking at some stock. There was a briskness in the air, and Gray Bess was taking her ease, lamely, among some riding horses and colts.

One of the stockmen turned to Hampton and said, "Will, what are you going to do with Gray Bess? Might as well put her to sleep with a .45, she'll freeze to death some morning this winter."

Mr. Hampton, almost as near the end of his westering as Bess, looked them all in the eye and said, "I'll take care of Bess this winter, and every other winter as long as she lives. See my house down there in the ranch cup? Bess and me come to this valley together, and she picked it out. I let her have her head and she stood stock still at that bend in the creek and that's where I cut my roof rafters."

"I'll say one thing for old Bess, she can stay on the trail of a bunch of Comanches better'n any horse I ever heard of —or used to could."

"She still can," said Hampton, "better'n any hound dog in the whole wide West."

As they were riding in about dusk some of the men thought they saw furtive forms stealing along the forest edge. They pulled up and watched.

"Comanches, by God!"

"A dozen of them!"

The first thing to do was to see to the security of their houses, for the red men might be planning an attack against the settlers' homes. Each man rode to his own place to post outlooks and ready their guns. Then they gathered again at Hampton's, where the Indians had been seen last. They kept up the watch all night but heard no sound, no shot, no signal.

In the gray of the morning, however, a savage lot of yelling and whooping broke loose from up toward the high pasture. The men grabbed their guns, mounted, and made off. They got to the upper pasture just in time to see the tail end of the Comanche band disappearing in the trees and heading toward the mountains. They had driven off all of Hampton's horses, including old Bess.

Hampton and his men followed hot on the trail. It was easy tracking such a large party, but not easy to come up to the thieving red men in spite of the handicap they had with Gray Bess. Hampton's party caught sight of the band on the mountainside two or three times, but they were not closing fast enough. Old Bess must have been taking a terrible punishment; they found blood on the gravel in several places.

"I'll follow them to Devil's Den," said Hampton, "and if they kill Bess in this drive I'll follow them to the Devil himself."

They pressed on and about midmorning came to where the trail forked. There was Bess tied to a tree, her feet bleeding and her limbs trembling.

"Now if old Bess can travel, she'll show us the way sure."

One trail led south to the canyon, the other west to the higher plateau.

"Cut that grass rope," ordered Hampton. "She'll show us which trail they took, though the signs around here point to the canyon. Could be a trick."

As soon as Bess was free she headed for the south trail to the canyon. Then she did a puzzling thing. She put out her forefeet and stopped short, wheeled, and galloped up to Hampton and laid her head on his shoulder. Then she turned and took the west trail up the mountain, making what time she could. She whinnied low from time to time but kept on the up trail.

Thus she led them on for miles, and when she could go no farther, she stopped and faced her master and his men.

She stumbled up to Hampton, laid her head over his shoulder for a great spell of hard breathing, and then dropped dead as a stone at his feet.

Hampton couldn't talk, but the look in his eyes said enough. After a respectful silence, one man said, "Gray Bess has led us up the wrong trail. If they was any Indians on this plateau we could see them."

"It's deeper than that," Hampton said. "Bess knows Indians. Why did she start toward the canyon first?"

Worn out and dejected, they backtrailed down the mountain and came again to where the trail forked. They stopped to look around. The canyon rim was not a quarter-mile away. They had not explored that trail very far till they all realized what a great debt they owed to old Gray Bess. The gun prints in the dirt and the many moccasin tracks and animal leavings showed plainly that the Comanches had laid an ambush for their small party. The raiding Indians had joined with a larger band in the canyon to wipe the settlers out. Realizing this, Gray Bess had led them away from the ambush and had saved their lives.

Recently I ran across a rhymed version of this story in the September 12, 1908, issue of the Gatesville *Messenger and Star Forum*. It was composed by Bessie Elam of Ohio, Texas. She had the story from W. W. Hampton himself, and her poem took me back to the time I sat in the doorway dreading to wash my feet and listening with rapt attention to one of Joe Sap's tales of the old times.

Tarantula Lore

LOIS BROCK

NOT MANY PEOPLE are fond of spiders. Grown men usually ignore them; small boys step on or torment them; women chase them with brooms and wash them down sinks. As the French entomologist, Henri Fabre, mildly expressed it, "The Spider has a bad name."[1] And the tarantula is the most maligned and most misunderstood of the entire spider kingdom. Because the docile, amiable tarantula of the southwestern United States is considered to be the fierce and deadly king of spiders, it has been a fascinating and rewarding study to trace its unmerited reputation back to its sources.

It all began in Europe in the Middle Ages. The dancing mania that accompanied the plagues and ravages of the twelfth through the fifteenth centuries was a contagious social dementia, easily spread by the fact that the medieval mind was "a morass of fears and superstitions."[2] Europeans in general thought the devil had a hoof in this mass hysteria, but the inhabitants of Taranto, in southern Italy, found a natural rather than a supernatural cause for the affliction. They blamed it on the bite of a certain large spider that was present in large numbers in the area.[3] Named *tarantula* after the village of Taranto, the spider supposedly had a narcotic poison that collected around the victim's heart, causing melancholy, stupor, and eventually death.[4] The sovereign cure was intense dancing; it was necessary to keep the bitten person active for twenty-four hours, or until he was completely exhausted and had sweated

41

out the poison. The very old and the very young were
difficult to treat because of the endurance required; over-
exertion was probably the reason for any deaths that resulted
from tarantism.[5]

Lively, exciting music was necessary for the stimulation of
the tarantists, and musicians were in such demand that guilds
of tarantula-players were formed. The passionate, rapidly
whirling dance that was most popular with the patients came
to be known as the tarantella.[6] The British naturalist, Theodore
Savory, gives this description of a patient's "cure":

> At first she lolled stupidly on a chair, while the instruments were
> playing some dull music. They touched, at length, the chord supposed
> to vibrate to her heart; and up she sprang with a hideous yell, staggered
> about the room like a drunken person, holding a handkerchief in both
> hands, raising them alternately, and moving in very true time. As the
> music grew brisker, her motions quickened, and she skipped about with
> great vigour and variety of steps, every now and then shrieking very loud.[7]

Epidemics were inevitable in the summer, when former
tarantists suffered relapses and the crowds of spectators were
infected with the insistent rhythm of the music and the fury
of the dance. The fact that tarantism was simply a dramatic
form of the dancing mania was obscured by the patients'
assertions that tarantulas had bitten them.[8] Savory claims that
the spider was simply a scapegoat for those who wanted to
engage in bacchanalian dancing and reveling.[9] Paracelsus
offered sound advice in the sixteenth century when he recommended immersion in cold water,[10] but by that time tarantism
had almost died out, leaving only the lively tarantella and a
bad name for spiders.[11]

Eleanore Flaig says, "At last the *Tarantati* was transferred
into a harmless festival known as the Women's Little Carnival,
and the spider, a one-time villain, crawled back into oblivion."[12]
The spider has remained a villain, however, and has transferred
his reputation to his brother spiders. Explorers and travelers
in other parts of the world applied the name and the reputation

of the tarantula to any large spiders, particularly those of the genus *Mygale* in America, and even to reptiles and lizards that looked venomous.[13] Strictly speaking, the true tarantula is the Italian wolf spider designated *Lycosa tarantula* by Linnaeus; it is a distant relative of our United States tarantula, which belongs to the family of "bird-eating spiders."[14] One English authority claims that the latter should be called the baboon or baviaan spider.[15] But in spite of protests from confused arachnologists, the name is well established by usage as the popular name for any large, hairy spider; it is used in German, Italian, Spanish, French, and Portuguese, as well as in English.[16] Neither the layman nor the tarantula seems to be bothered by the overlapping of names.

Except in literary form, the legend of Taranto did not survive the transplantation to America. On a visit to the States after the Mexican War, Big-Foot Wallace found that people doubted his factual stories, but believed his whoppers. When one skeptical young lady refused to believe that he had seen forty thousand horses in one drove,

> "Well, then," said I, "maybe you won't believe me when I tell you there is a sort of spider in Texas as big as a peck measure, the bite of which can only be cured by music."
> "Oh, yes," she answered, "I believe that's all so, for I have read about them in a book."[17]

New superstitions evolved about the tarantula in the Southwest. My father recalls, "I have heard old-timers say a tarantula would spit in your eyes, and you would go blind. When tarantulas are out crawling around it is a sign of rain."[18] One curious reversal of the European legend is the belief that the tarantula's bite cures insanity.[19] This seems to be the only example of the medicinal benefits of the tarantula's bite, although other spiders are believed to bring luck and cure various diseases.[20]

The general belief about the tarantula in the Southwest is

that its bite is almost always fatal. This has been perpetuated by the tall tales and the hearsay about the spider, as well as by the doubt of arachnologists themselves. Consider the contribution to folklore of the showman who took his tarantulas to New York City and enlightened its citizens by offering them a look at "two of the wildest, most venomous Mexican tarantulas ever seen in captivity"[21] for only a dime. He thoughtfully kept them behind strong wire screens to prevent an attack on the spectators. Claiming that they grew to be six feet across, he explained that their name came from a famous South American Indian, old Chief Taran Tula, "one of the fiercest most murderous Indians ever known in this hemisphere, who tied his captives in spider dens."[22]

Some personal adventures are only slightly less fantastic than such tall tales. George W. Tuttle's financial venture in tarantulas shows that he was a shrewd businessman, but a naïve naturalist. Stranded in Pasadena, California, by the collapse of the real estate boom in the 1890's, he turned to collecting tarantulas for a wholesale house, at five cents per spider. The business in mounted tarantulas and similar souvenirs of early California was such a lucrative one that he soon started his own wholesale business, supplying shops in the United States and England with boxes labeled "Great Curiosity! California tarantula!"[23]

Despite his close contact with the spiders, Tuttle never lost his conviction that they were "vicious brigands of the mesa," with fangs "dripping with virulent poison."[24] Such a description would have increased the retail value of his merchandise, but he writes of his adventures in the California tarantula fields over a quarter of a century later, when there is no need for exaggeration. Evidently he never questioned the rumors about tarantulas:

The bite is undoubtedly very dangerous. In the early days of Pasadena, one man was bitten. The bite did not prove fatal but it was a long time before the man recovered from its effects. I had narrow escapes but was never bitten, for which I am devoutly thankful. . . . There is real danger in collecting tarantulas. It is the tarantula that crawls upon you unseen that is dangerous. . . . One tarantula was taken from my back, another sought to find a snug refuge in the leg of my trousers. . . . My neighbor had terrible tarantula dreams the first night or two that we were out but these soon passed away and he was as self-possessed when handling a particularly vicious specimen as any man living could be.[25]

The sale of California's insects and arachnids was a thriving business until the supply ran out. Considering the reputation of the tarantula, this exploitation must have been a blessing to the citizens of Southern California. Tuttle averaged a hundred spiders per day, including large numbers of males during the mating season,[26] and Charles F. Holder, another chronicler of the industry, says that one firm alone mounted thousands of tarantulas every year.[27] He adds:

> The average tourist thinks it necessary to carry home something as a souvenir. . . . I sometimes think that tourists wish to convey the idea to their less fortunate friends that they have been traveling in a dangerous country, and so send or take back home the poisonous insects as evidence of it. In any event, there is an ever-increasing demand for them. . . . The tarantula trade is, perhaps, the most important; the huge hairy creatures being more repulsive than others are consequently more in demand.[28]

Live tarantulas, however, are treated with the respect and caution that a rattlesnake or a Gila monster merits. The typical reaction is that of the automobile driver who leaped out without stopping his car when he saw a large tarantula on the floorboard. In spite of his injuries and his wrecked car, he felt thankful at having "escaped."[29]

The tragic stories of tarantula victims are nearly always told by someone who knew someone else who knew of the case, as in this example given by W. J. Baerg, a noted authority on tarantulas:

> Mr. Swift told me that an acquaintance, Mr. Steele, attended the funeral of a little girl. At the grave the heartbroken mother related that

her daughter had been bitten by a large tarantula, and after indescribable suffering had died on the following day.[30]

John H. Comstock, an American entomologist, says that there are no authenticated cases of tarantula bites;[31] Baerg mentions a few cases of illness and death, resulting from the bites of tropical tarantulas in the United States.[32] The black "banana tarantulas" are thought to be more deadly than rattlesnakes, here in the United States as well as in their native South America.[33] Although the southwestern tarantula is the heavyweight of North American spiders, its next of kin in the tropics, the banana tarantulas and the tree-dwelling bird-spiders, are larger by at least an inch.[34] The English naturalist, W. H. Hudson, describes the Argentine tarantula as "a gigantic cockroach mounted on stilts";[35] he warns that it is high-spirited and touchy, and is not to be treated with contempt:

> One [species] is extremely abundant on the pampas, the Mygale fusca, a veritable monster, covered with dark brown hair, and called in the vernacular *aranea peluda*—hairy spider. In the hot month of December these spiders take to roaming about on the open plain, and are then everywhere seen traveling in a straight line with a slow even pace. They are very great in attitudes, and when one is approached it immediately throws itself back, like a pugilist preparing for an encounter, and stands up so erect on its four hind feet that the under surface of its body is displayed. . . . I do not think any creature, however stupid, could mistake its meaning when it stands suddenly up, a figure horribly grotesque; then, dropping down on all eights, charges violently forwards. Their long, shiny black, sickle-shaped falces are dangerous weapons. I knew a native woman who had been bitten on the leg, and who, after fourteen years, still suffered at intervals acute pains in the limb.[36]

A juxtaposition of Big-Foot Wallace and Alexander E. Sweet shows the different attitudes toward the tarantula in the early days of the Southwest. Wallace believed that its bite was worse than that of the rattlesnake. As a member of the Mier Expedition, he saw several persons who were fatally bitten; one of the Texans' guards at Monterrey was bitten, "and although the Mexicans tried many kinds of 'remedios' to relieve him, they all failed, and he died in a few hours."[37] The Mexicans believed that the tarantula's bite would kill a horse in ten minutes.[38]

Sweet, on the other hand, has nothing but sympathy for the slandered spider. He describes the appearance and habits of the trap-door spider, which is closely related to the tarantula of the Southwest. The frontier Indian, the horse-thief, and the Mexican raider were all acquainted with the spider and considered its nocturnal life worthy of imitation.[39] Though wise and cautious, the tarantula has its faults:

When insulted or injured in any way,—sat down upon, for instance,— he will bite the first soft place he can find, exuding a vicious substance said to be as fatal as the poison of a rattlesnake or the effects of frontier whiskey. I think this is another slander, for I have never met a man who was fatally bitten by a tarantula. "Tarantula-juice" is a favorite appellation in Texas for the worst kind of whiskey, and probably on the principle that "a hair of the dog," etc., whiskey is the only antidote successfully used in cases of tarantula bite. I have heard it stated,— I give the statement for what it is worth, probably about five cents on the dollar,—that an old Indian who lived on the Nueces loved the antidote so much, that he carried around a tame tarantula, made it convenient to get bitten close to a grocery, exhibited the tarantula as proof, and howled around until he was gratuitously irrigated with whiskey by the humane storekeeper.[40]

Because of lack of evidence and out of respect for the size of the spider, arachnologists have advised until recently that tarantulas should be avoided. But the work of investigators like Baerg has changed the scientific, if not the popular, attitude. When "an intelligent young man told me that his brother had been bitten by a tarantula and had died as a result a few days later,"[41] Baerg began to experiment, in the manner of Fabre, on guinea pigs and mice. He then tried the poison on himself and found that the only effect was the pain of the bites, similar to the sensation of pin stabs. He points out, however, that some people are very sensitive to some animal poisons,[42] and thus it is difficult to generalize about the effect of tarantula bites. The tarantula is harmless when compared to the black widow, which has a larger poison sac and a much more virulent poison.[43] But the reaction always depends on the person bitten; even bee and wasp stings are sometimes fatal. Allergy, secondary infection, and the mental reaction must be taken into account.

In connection with the spider's bite, the loss of horses' and mules' hoofs in Mexico and Central America is attributed to the tarantula. The superstition maintains that the spider climbs over the hoof and cuts off the hair in a narrow strip around the leg, for use in its nest. No damage results unless the tarantula is disturbed and bites. Other versions say that the cutting of the hair causes the hoof to fall off, whether or not the spider bites, and that the tarantula's urine is the damaging agent.[44] The hoof losses have been traced to infection caused by bacilli[45]—a prosaic explanation in comparison with that of folklore.

Even if the tarantula did not have a name that connotes horror and peril, from the poetry of John Fiske to the philosophy of Nietzsche,[46] its appearance would lead people to believe the worst. But the tarantula's formidable appearance and the pugilistic attitude described by Hudson are devices for defense, rather than indications of viciousness. By means of the hairs that completely cover its body, it relies on its delicate sense of touch for finding its prey and the opposite sex. Tarantula eyes can distinguish degrees of light intensity only.[47] Despite its extremely limited vision, it is popularly believed to attack human beings by jumping from a distance of twelve or fifteen feet.[48] South American tarantulas are called antelopes, because of their alleged jumping habit.[49]

The size of the tarantula, like the length of the jump, varies with the speaker's imagination. Newspaper accounts always describe them as huge or enormous, and anyone who kills a tarantula usually rates a front-page story. Many miners and prospectors who have shaken them out of their blankets and boots in the morning have sworn that they were as big as saucers, or as large as a dinner plate and standing a foot high.[50] The average adult tarantula in the Southwest has a one- or two-inch body,[51] with a leg spread of four or five inches.[52] The emotional reaction of a sudden encounter, plus the psychological value of exaggeration, accounts for the tradition of huge tarantulas.

In the early days of the Southwest, tarantulas were utilized as a means of entertainment. The young boys who were not working for the California taxidermists were staging tarantula wrestling matches. Mexican boys in Baja California bet their centavos on their favorites, pitted against each other in makeshift arenas of tin pans. An unidentified traveler in that area reported in the *Detroit Free Press:*

> When the hideous-looking things were thrown in the pan they eyed each other for a moment and then clutched like a couple of tigers, while the Mexican youths yelled words of encouragement to their favorites. From the comments that I heard I took it that there were fine points to the game that I did not understand. All I saw was a horrible, hairy ball from which protruded in all directions a number of hairy legs that suddenly grew still, as death claimed the victims.[53]

Cowboys also played the tarantulas, in the days before speculation in the stock market and televised fights. W. D. Woodson's description of the pastime makes a sinister picture:

> In the glow of the campfire, two tiny gladiators were pitted against one another. Bets were made, the cheering began, and the small creatures battled to the death. . . . The distant coyotes sounded their weird call; the prairie owl made love to the moon; the nighthawk patrolled her long stretch. The cowboys, seated like witches plotting a deed of horror, eagerly watched the agony of two cannibals whose code was the law of the jungle.[54]

Thus, the history of the tarantula involves distortion of truth and exaggeration of danger, because of man's reliance on his senses rather than his reason and because of his vivid imagination. Authorities on tarantulas now recommend them as excellent pets, more even-tempered than cats or dogs,[55] but the tarantula continues to be one of those creatures killed on sight because it looks dangerous or because someone has said it is deadly. Man will go on believing what he wants to believe. John Crompton tells of a friend who asked, "*Is* there any cure for the bite of a tarantula?" When Crompton told him the truth, "he smiled to himself and spoke no more about it, and I perceived that I had lost forever any standing that I might have had with him as an authority on spiders."[56]

1. J. Henri Fabre, *Insect Adventures*, trans. Alexander Teixeira de Mattos, retold by Louise Seymour Hasbrouck (Yonkers-on-Hudson: World Book Co., 1918), p. 209.

2. Eleanore Flaig, "Dancing for the Gods of Evil," *Travel*, LXXXIII (October, 1944), 22.

3. *Ibid.*

4. "Tarantism" and "tarantula," *Webster's New Collegiate Dictionary* (Springfield, Mass.: G. & C. Merriam Co., 1956).

5. Flaig, *op. cit.*, p. 22.

6. "Tarantella," *New English Dictionary*, Vol. IX (1901).

7. Theodore H. Savory, *The Biology of Spiders* (New York: Macmillan Co., 1928), p. 127.

8. Flaig, *op. cit.*, pp. 22-23.

9. Savory, *op. cit.*, pp. 127-28.

10. Flaig, *op. cit.*, p. 22.

11. Frederick Drimmer, ed., *The Animal Kingdom* (Garden City: Doubleday, 1954), III, 1738.

12. Flaig, *op. cit.*, p. 23.

13. "Tarantula," *New English Dictionary*.

14. John Henry Comstock, *The Spider Book* (Garden City: Doubleday, Page, 1913), p. 228.

15. Quoted by W. J. Baerg, "Tarantulas as They Are," *Today's Health*, XXXII (August, 1954), 19.

16. W. J. Baerg, "The Poisons of Scorpions and Spiders," *Natural History*, XLII (June, 1938), 47.

17. John C. Duval, *The Adventures of Big-Foot Wallace* (Austin: Steck Co., 1947), pp. 275-76.

18. Personal communication from W. E. Brock, Seminole, Texas.

19. Oren Arnold, *Wild Life in the Southwest* (Dallas: Banks, Upshaw, 1935), p. 171.

20. John Crompton, *The Life of the Spider* (New York: New American Library, 1950), p. 181; Mary V. Hood, *Outdoor Hazards, Real and Fancied* (New York: Macmillan Co., 1955), p. 90.

21. Arnold, *op. cit.*, p. 170.

22. *Ibid.*

23. George W. Tuttle, "Making a Living out of Insects," *Outing,* LXXIX (November, 1921), 75-76.

24. *Ibid.*, p. 76.

25. *Ibid.*, p. 93.

26. *Ibid.*, pp. 76, 94.

27. Charles F. Holder, "A Singular Industry in the Poisonous Insects of California," *Scientific American,* LXXXIV (March 30, 1901), 202.

28. *Ibid.*

29. A newspaper account cited by Baerg, "The Poisons of Scorpions and Spiders," p. 47.

30. W. J. Baerg, "Tarantulas as Pets," *Nature Magazine,* IX (March, 1927), 173.

31. Comstock, *op. cit.*, p. 228.

32. Baerg, "Tarantulas as They Are," p. 58.

33. Baerg, "Tarantulas as Pets," p. 173.

34. "Spiders and Their Habits," *Scientific American Supplement,* LXXVI (August 9, 1913), 94.

35. W. H. Hudson, *The Naturalist in La Plata* (London: Chapman & Hall, 1892), p. 179.

36. *Ibid.*, pp. 191-92.

37. Duval, *op. cit.*, pp. 28, 183.

38. *Ibid.*, p. 28.

39. Alexander E. Sweet and J. Armoy Knox, *On a Mexican Mustang through Texas* (Hartford: S. S. Scranton & Co., 1885), pp. 139-40.

40. *Ibid.*, pp. 140-41.

41. W. J. Baerg, "Regarding the Habits of Tarantulas and the Effects of Their Poison," *Scientific Monthly,* XIV (May, 1922), 486.

42. Baerg, "Tarantulas as They Are," p. 58.

43. Hood, *op. cit.*, p. 91.

44. Baerg, "The Poisons of Scorpions and Spiders," p. 46.

45. *Ibid;* Hood, *op. cit.*, p. 92.

46. Baerg, "The Poisons of Scorpions and Spiders," p. 46.

47. Baerg, "Tarantulas as Pets," p. 173.

48. Brock, *op. cit.*

49. Baerg, "Tarantulas as Pets," p. 173.

50. C. E. Hutchinson, "Habits of the Tarantula," *Scientific American,* XCVIII (January 11, 1908), 23.

51. Natt N. Dodge and Herbert S. Zim, *The American Southwest* (New York: Simon & Schuster, 1955), p. 67.

52. Drimmer, *op. cit.*, p. 1738.

53. Quoted in "A Mexican Sport," *Current Literature*, XXXII (January, 1902), 91.

54. Weldon Dwight Woodson, "In Search of California Spiders," *Travel*, LXVI (February, 1936), 41.

55. Alexander I. Petrunkevitch, quoted in "Spider Man," *Newsweek*, XXIII (June 12, 1944), 92; Baerg, "Tarantulas as They Are," p. 54.

56. Crompton, *op. cit.*, p. 56.

The Mystery of the Five Graves

JOHN C. MYERS

WITHIN the highway right-of-way between Carrizo Springs and Eagle Pass lie five unidentified graves, neatly grouped. The burial plot is enclosed by a chain-link fence, and each grave is marked by a plain white wooden cross. During the midday heat, a pair of gnarled mesquite trees cast an uncertain shade over the spot. The scene is one of peace and quiet. A short distance away, the highway crosses a dry creek bed.

There is something about an unidentified grave that creates mystery and excites the imagination. It is a riddle asking for a solution. Now place five such graves together, and the mystery is compounded. How did five graves come to be in such isolation, away from a proper burial ground? Who are the people who lie in the graves? How did they meet their end, and why were they buried at this particular spot? These questions puzzle the passers-by, for the uninscribed crosses give no clues at all.

But there must be a reason for the grouping of the graves at this lonely spot. Surely someone can supply the answers. My search reveals that no article has been printed concerning the five graves. The next best thing to do would be to consult the oldest residents of the area. Surely a day so spent would turn up some kind of reliable information.

I sought out Uncle Ed Walton, who, venerable and ageless, has an answer ready for those who want to know how old he is: "By God, I'm old enough to sleep by myself." Testy though he was, he readily agreed to talk to me about the five graves.

"The way it came to me was something like this," said Uncle Ed. Here is his story, not told in his words. Among the first arrivals who settled at Eagle Pass in the early days was a family by the name of Larkin. In this frontier town, misfortune followed misfortune for the Larkins. Finally the family decided to give up everything and move to East Texas, where relatives lived.

The family now included five boys and four girls. They started out early one morning traveling in a wagon drawn by mules. Mr. Larkin was determined to leave behind forever this severe land which had dealt so unkindly with him. But he and four of his sons never quite made it.

The second day out, while they were stopping for a noon-day rest, one of their dogs dragged into camp an armadillo which it had killed. The family decided to clean the animal and take the meat along to be cooked for the evening meal. Only Mr. Larkin and the four oldest boys could stomach the strong meat of the armadillo. About two hours later the five were seized by violent stomach cramps. Despite the efforts of Mrs. Larkin, the five who had partaken of the armadillo meat died in agony. The next morning, passers-by helped bury the dead and assisted Mrs. Larkin in resuming her journey. The crosses that mark the graves are still there by the road for everyone to see.

"That could have happened, except for one thing," said I. "Armadillo meat is not poisonous. Many people still eat and enjoy the flesh of the armadillo."

"I know it ain't poisonous," said Uncle Ed. "But if the guts of the animal are ripped poison can come out, and when the dog killed that armadillo it maybe bit into the animal a little too deep and let loose the poison that spoiled the meat."

I turned for verification to an old friend of Uncle Ed's who had also heard the recital. Yes, it was about the way he had heard it, except that it was a family of Mexicans returning to Mexico, and the thing that did the killing was tainted javelina meat.

Another account was given me by an elderly resident who is a former county judge. Many years ago, a family by the name of Burleson owned a farm on Peña Creek, near the site of the five graves. The creek was then flowing the year round, and the Burleson farm was well improved. As was customary in those days, residents in the rural areas had their family burial plots located on their own property.

The five crosses mark the graves of Mr. Burleson and four children, who, according to one version, died during a scarlet fever epidemic. Others say that the deaths resulted from eating spoiled venison. When the present highway was built, it passed very close to the family burial plot of the Burlesons, but left it undisturbed.

A resident of a house near the scene of the five crosses had the following story to relate:

"We moved to this place about twenty years ago. The people we bought from told us the story of what happened.

"A loaded truck going toward Eagle Pass went out of control and smashed into a buggy, killing all the occupants. In the buggy was a family of Mexicans, two adults and three children, who were on a trip to San Antonio.

"No, the crosses do not mark the graves of the people who were killed—they were buried somewhere else. The crosses are the result of an old Spanish custom. When a traveler is killed on a road or highway, it is customary to mark the spot with a mound of rocks by the wayside. Later, a wooden cross is placed on the mound. Then on special days, relatives and friends may hang wreaths or garlands of flowers on the arms of the cross in memory of the departed. Those crosses down there mark the spot where the highway accident took place."

Leaving the house, I mused upon the plausibility of what

I had heard. Could there be any more solutions? I had one more stop to make in my quest.

The home of Eugenio Canales was in Piedras Negras, on a bluff overlooking a bend in the Rio Grande. By way of answer to my query, Eugenio led me around his house to a patio and motioned me to a comfortable seat. There, beneath the shade of several large hackberry trees, I knew I would find the answer, because Eugenio and his father before him had worked the better part of their lives as cowboys on the ranches of the area where the graves are located. Although Eugenio was straight and erect, his legs were bent and bowed from a lifetime spent in the saddle. His face was weathered and tanned, and his gnarled and wrinkled hands resembled limbs of an old mesquite tree. Sitting down beside me, he began his tale.

"Sí, sí, I remember well what happened. I was a *chamaco* [boy] at the time, but *mi papá* told me the story. That was long, long time ago, before the fence came, open country, you say. *Mi papá* was riding for the *patrón* who worked many men, and he had a big remuda and he handled many cattle. It was when many *bandidos* raided up from Mexico.

"One day while the men were holding wild cattle on the Nueces River bottom, a bunch of *bandidos mejicanos* rode up and tried to break up remuda, run off horses. But *mi papá* and the *patrón* and the other men surrounded the *bandidos* and captured them. The *patrón* did not know what to do with the *bandidos*. There was no law at the time. Finally they decided to hang half of them and let the others go with a warning never to come back to that side. This was done and the five remaining *bandidos* were started toward the border. They have their guns and sombreros taken away, so they cannot remain long over there."

I said, "Then the five crosses are over the graves of the five bandits who were hanged and buried there?"

"Oh, no, no, señor, not quite," replied Eugenio. "You see, when the five were turned loose, they have much hate for the gringo. They lose much face and they swear that they will kill the first people they see. They ride about fifteen miles toward the big river. It is late at night. They come over a hill and see a stream below, and there is an Indian camp located on the bank. All in the camp are asleep. They dismount and crawl toward the camp. They still have their knives and it take only a few minutes to cut the throats of five Indians. They crawl back to the horses, and by riding hard they are back in Mexico a little after sunup the next day. Then the Indians were buried where they were killed. It was close to a small stream or arroyo, called Peña Creek."

Was this the solution to the mystery? I looked up and saw a white-winged dove glide in through the branches and exchange places with its mate on a nest. On an adjacent limb, a pair of half-grown doves watched in silence. The old man's eyes followed mine. "That pair of *palomas blancas* come every summer to my trees. Always raise six or eight little ones. *Muy bien!* Take me six or eight years do same thing."

I leaned back in comfort. A cool breeze was blowing off the river. The lengthening shadows were about to melt into dusk. I thought of the five crosses and the day I had spent in trying to learn their secret. Had I found the answer? Was the mystery solved? Probably not. But I had seen, close at hand, an illustration of the need of people to explain a local phenomenon and their willingness to accept not very plausible stories in their effort to do so. In this way legends get started.

The Petroleum Geologist: A Folk Image

MODY C. BOATRIGHT

THE STATUS of the petroleum geologist during the first thirty years of this century was somewhat below that of hero. In the rejoicing of a community when oil came, he was likely to be overshadowed if not forgotten. The oil field that he mapped was not named for him.

Samuel W. Tait complains of a "convention of anonymity about all oil discoveries which is observed by all writers," who, he says, fail to disclose that back of every big discovery "was a single man, usually a geologist, with the courage to fight for his convictions at the risk of losing his professional standing."[1] There is no reason, however, for believing that there has been a conspiracy on the part of reporters and popular historians to belittle the role of geology in the development of the oil industry. They brought to their writing certain presuppositions about the qualities which gave interest and significance to the events reported. That is, they assumed that they knew what their readers wanted: conflict, humor, sentiment, action, and the like. These were the qualities they looked for, and the qualities they failed to find in the work of the geologist. His conflicts were conflicts of ideas. His battles were waged within a small group, not in the open forum. If they came to the attention of the reporter at all, he did not know how to make a feature story of them. The result of his writing was more to confirm the popular ideas of geology than to impart accurate ones.

The attitude of the farmer or rancher toward the geologist

was ambivalent. If he was known to be looking for oil, he was welcome. If questioned about the prospects, he was evasive, but if you watched him carefully, you would see that he kept coming back to a certain place, and that would be where it looked best for oil. If his report was unfavorable and nobody offered to lease your land, he probably didn't know very much about his business. If his report was favorable and somebody leased your land and put down a well and didn't get oil, the geologist was unquestionably right, but the driller was incompetent or dishonest. Maybe he had passed the oil sand without knowing; maybe he didn't drill to the specified depth, made a false report, and collected his money; or more likely he was bought off by a rival company, probably Standard Oil, and plugged the well.

Nobody knows when the term "rock hound" was first applied to the geologist, but it might well have come from the country folk. M. G. Cheney noted that the people who watched him work thought he roamed over an area in the manner of a coon dog looking for a scent, and when they saw him return to a point of reference, they thought of a coon dog returning to the place where he had lost the trail.[2]

And Charles Gould reports the following story:

> . . . an old farmer in southern Kansas was surprised and concerned to see two men with surveying instruments out on a rocky hill in his pasture. He asked a neighbor if he knew who the intruders were.
>
> "Oh, them's rock hounds," said the neighbor. "They've been chasing that ledge of limestone clear across the country. Yesterday Bill Jones, he started to chase 'em off'n his place, but they told him they was huntin' for oil, so he let 'em stay. Says he thought if they could locate oil on his farm, he'd better let 'em do it.[3]

A hound is a smart animal, so if "rock hound" originated among country folk, it had for them no derogatory implications.

Among oilmen it probably did. Operators were slow to recognize the validity of geological science, or at least of its usefulness to them. Their saying, "Geology never filled an oil tank," persisted long after it had ceased to be true.[4] John Gayley in his early Texas years said that the only reliable geologist was Dr. Drill.[5] Another successful wildcatter used to say,[6] "To hell with geology. Let's go dig an oil well."* Benjamin Coyle thought a geologist's favorable report was like a shot of dope. "It just spurts him [the oilman] to go ahead ... you don't like to go out and start anything if somebody don't give you a shot in the arm." This was the chief value of geology. He had some mighty nice friends who were geologists and he used to tell them that if he ever found a guy that knew as much as they did, he was going to marry him. At least, "he'll think I'm married to him, I'll stick so close to him."[7]

One way to belittle geology was to give fantastic accounts of how decisions on drilling locations were made. One old-time oilman told Charles Gould that "his favorite way of locating oil was to tie a tin can on a dog's tail and start the dog on a run across the prairies. Where the can came off, there he would drill."[8] And Lew Allen reported in 1922 that "although admitting that most of the recent strikes have been located by geologists, many old-time operators affect to scorn the 'rock hounds' and use their own original methods." He quotes one man as saying,

Not that I don't believe in geologists. I always use one. I'm that big a fool. Pay him $50.00 a day to chip rocks and write reports. But when I get ready to start, I take a Negro and blindfold him, turn him around three times, and let him throw a silver dollar as far as he can. Where the dollar falls, if I can find it, is the spot where I drill.[9]

One operator was told by his geologist that he had located the well off the structure. His reply was, "Well, skid the structure over a little."[10]

*This attitude, however, was not universal. The Rio Bravo Oil Company, a subsidiary of the Southern Pacific Railroad, was the first oil company to set up a geological department. The department was organized by E. T. Dumble in 1897. (See Edgar W. Owens, "Remarks on the History of American Petroleum Geology," *Journal of the Washington Academy of Sciences*, XLIX [July, 1959], 256-60.)

The drillers and tool dressers and roughnecks were as con-temptuous as their employers. "The average fellow in the oil field," reports one geologist, would say, "There goes one of those scientists," or "Here comes another one of those scientist so and soes."[11] Ex-driller Billy Bryant spoke for many of his trade when he said that if he were a big oilman he would hire a geologist, one of the best he could find. "And every time I got me a section of land, I'd let him go out and make a location, and if he made the location on the south corner, I'd go to the north corner and make a well."[12]

Such appraisals of the geologist may be accounted for in part by the fact that the early discoveries were made without his help. The pioneer seekers of petroleum had little need for geology. They looked for oil springs or oil or gas seepages, clearly visible on the surface. "Nearly every producing region (*petroleum province*)," says A. T. Levorsen, "was discovered as a result of drilling prompted by the recognition of nearby surface or subsurface showings of gas, oil, or asphalt."[13] Among the subsurface indications the most important was the encoun-tering of oil or gas in wells drilled for water.

Two epoch-making discoveries will come to mind imme-diately. Drake drilled near an oil spring. Once the province was discovered, geology was able to trace it into West Virginia. Patillo Higgins' interest in Spindletop began when he noticed gas seeps. The well proved to be on a salt dome; this led to a search for other salt domes, but in this search science was not especially helpful until the introduction of geophysical instru-ments. Before that time, a layman could do about as well as a scientist.

Equally important in accounting for the tardy recognition of geology was the practical man's contempt for the theorizer, the doer's contempt for the thinker. Even before Drake's dis-covery in 1859 a Canadian geologist had formulated a struc-tural theory to account for a series of oil seepages, a theory which by the end of the 1860's had been elaborated and accepted by many geologists. But this early work was done by academic geologists more interested in advancing their science than in finding oil.[14] It was not until 1883 that the first consulting petroleum geologist, I. C. White, opened his office. Writing in 1892 he expressed gratification "in having assisted in removing this stigma [expressed in the saying "Geology never filled an oil tank"] from our profession."[15] But the stigma was not to be completely removed for a long time. As late as 1952 one successful independent operator felt that a geologist's report should be studied with great caution. The geologist is a scientist, accustomed to thinking in scientific terms, and if he finds "even a suspicion of a structure . . . he, perhaps unconsciously, takes the position that a well ought to be drilled to find out what's there."[16] In brief, there is an inherent conflict of interest. The operator wants oil; the geologist wants information.

Yet in the widely publicized classical examples of geological error, the advice has been *not* to drill. Any geologist with long experience in petroleum will confess to errors in the interpretation of data, and he knows the uncertainty of finding oil even on the most favorable structure. Charles Gould, who has been called the father of petroleum geology in the Southwest, and who certainly found his share of oil, used to say that any anticline was worth drilling but he knew that not every anticline contained oil.[17] Some of the Gulf Coast salt domes showed no surface outcropping by which they could be defined, nor did stratigraphic traps such as the ones underlying the great East Texas field. In the Mexia region Colonel Humphreys disposed of a part of his holdings upon the recommendation of a geologist, who said it was not on the structure. When the company that had acquired the leases brought in a well, Humphreys wired the geologist, who was in New York, to hurry back to Texas. They had skidded the structure over.[18] Wallace Pratt, one of the great geologists, who had much to do with the success of the Humble Company, had had the same opinion, but he solved the geological problem in time for his company to make profitable leases. He seems to have miscalculated the angle of the fault, and thus oil was produced on what on the surface appeared to be a downhill side.[19]

The successes of geology were taken for granted. It was the failures that passed into tradition.

These failures have received embodiment in a widely diffused narrative. A local citizen, hoping to strengthen the economy of the community, and/or a wildcatter, hoping to make money, becomes convinced that there is oil under certain terrain. The reasons for this conviction vary all the way from religious faith to a new and unorthodox geological theory. A geological opinion is obtained, sometimes from a "government" or "state" geologist, sometimes from a consulting geologist, sometimes from the staff of a big oil company. The report is emphatically unfavorable, and often the geologist offers to drink all the oil found.

But bolstered by his own theory or by his mystic faith, and supported by the local citizens, the wildcatter moves in his equipment and proceeds to drill. The condemnation of the location by geology, however, makes it exceedingly difficult to find the risk capital necessary to finance the drilling. The first attempt to drill a well is usually a failure, either because the equipment is inferior or because the producing sand has been missed by a few feet or a few hundred feet. Additional money has to be raised, but the local people have lost faith and refuse to make further investments. Every legitimate method of financing is resorted to. Finally, when money and credit are down to the last dollar, the well comes in. A new field or perhaps a whole new province has been discovered. The big companies that have refused to help finance the well rush in and lease land at rentals a hundred or a thousand times those prevailing before the discovery. The geologist, instead of drinking oil as promised, says, "Ah!"

This is the pattern, the archetype, in which the popular imagination, aided by popular journalism, tends to fashion the event, though not every element is present in every version. It is not entirely without truth, but upon investigation of particular versions the truth proves to be somewhat more complex than the mythic pattern and somewhat less disparaging to geology.

Although oil and gas seeps had been known to exist in Texas since 1543, in 1900 there was only one oil field, Corsicana, operating in the state, and its production in that year was only 829,544 barrels. On January 10, 1901, the Lucas gusher came in, and by the end of the year the Spindletop field had produced 3,593,113 barrels. The next year its production was 17,420,049 barrels, and Texas took rank among the leading oil producing states.[20]

C. A. Warner cites 1892 as the date and Spindletop as the place of the first attempt in Texas to utilize geology in the search for oil,[21] implying an acceptance of Patillo Higgins' lifelong claim that he had geological reasons, other than surface gas, for believing that oil could be found. Higgins had studied a publication of the United States Geological Survey, and had perhaps identified the low mound four miles south of Beaumont as an anticline; but unless it is among his unpublished papers, he has left no detailed account of his theory. He did believe that gas in contact with sand and shale would cause them to turn to rock, and thus form a roof for an oil trap.[22] But if the memory of one of his fellow-townsmen may be trusted, he also witched the hill with a peach limb.[23]

Captain Lucas, who took over when three attempts to penetrate the quicksand had failed and Higgins was at the end of his resources, may also be said to have been prompted by geology. As a mining engineer employed by a salt company in Louisiana, he had encountered sulphur and showings of oil in association with salt. He correctly surmised that the low mounds on the coastal plains might be subterranean plugs of crystallized salt which might form oil traps.

Aside from Higgins and Lucas, four professional geologists passed judgment on the hill as a prospect for oil. Two judgments were favorable and two were unfavorable.

After the failure of the drilling contractor to attain the specified depth, Savage Brothers of West Virginia offered to put down a well for a 10 per cent royalty. They were advised by a "practical" geologist named Otley. Otley belonged to the trend, or vein, as opposed to the structural, school of geology. He held that deposits were in veins running from mountain ranges. He predicated a vein running from the Rocky Mountains to the Gulf of Mexico, thus providing an abundance of oil on the Coastal Plain. But in spite of Otley's conviction, Savage Brothers gave up their holdings upon their second failure to drill through the quicksand.[24]

Higgins wrote to Robert Dumble, chief state geologist of Texas, asking him to come to Beaumont and investigate the mound. Dumble could not come, but sent his chief assistant, William Kennedy. Kennedy evidently took the assignment seriously. He could find no reason for believing that oil would be found. He said that rock impervious to oil must overlie an oil deposit, and that he had found that a well in Beaumont, only four miles away, had been drilled to a depth of 1,400 feet without encountering such rock. He thought Higgins was wasting his money, and to protect others who might be inclined to invest, he published an article in the Beaumont paper.[25]

When Captain Lucas had taken over and exhausted his resources, C. Willard Hayes, of the United States Geological Survey, appeared in Beaumont, apparently upon his own initiative. He said that there was no precedent of oil's being found in the unconsolidated sands, shales, and gravels characteristic of the Coastal Plain. And like Kennedy, he added subsurface evidence. In search of artesian water, the city of Galveston, some sixty miles from Beaumont, had drilled a well 3,070 feet, and had encountered nothing to indicate the presence of oil.[26]

The fourth geologist to express a judgment on Spindletop was Dr. William Battle Phillips, professor of field geology at the University of Texas and director of the Texas State Mineral Survey. He came to Beaumont, inspected the area, and talked to Lucas. He decided that the chances for oil were good. He suggested that Lucas approach Guffey and Galey, an oil firm of Pittsburgh which had holdings in Corsicana. To make the approach easier he gave Lucas a letter of introduction to John Galey.[27] Galey at that time had little faith in geology, and it was doubtful whether Phillips' letter was decisive. Yet it was a geologist who brought Lucas and Galey together and led to Guffey and Galey's financing the discovery well.

But for many years Phillips was forgotten and Kennedy and Hayes were remembered, and geology was said to have failed initially in Texas; and for that reason it was not employed in localities where it could have been useful.[28]

The Commonwealth of Massachusetts had filed a suit against Edgar B. Davis of Luling, Texas. Davis had lived in Luling since 1922, but the commonwealth maintained that he had been a citizen of Massachusetts until 1926 and that he owed the state income taxes on a sum estimated as high as twelve million dollars. When a lawyer called on one citizen of Luling in search of evidence that Davis was not a legal resident of Texas, he was promptly informed that any man who said Davis was not a bona fide citizen of Luling, Texas, was a lying son of a bitch.[29]

This was hardly legal evidence, and Massachusetts eventually obtained a judgment; but it is indicative of what the people of Luling and the surrounding country thought of Davis. He was emphatically a hero. Not only had he brought wealth to the community by discovering oil, but he had distributed his personal fortune in giving generous bonuses to his employees, in sponsoring art, in building community clubhouses, and in

chartering and endowing the Luling Foundation for the better-
ment of agriculture. And in the search for oil he had personally
spent considerably more than a million dollars.

The people of Luling, in recounting his exploits to Stanley
Walker,[30] repeated the legend of his singlehanded struggle to
find oil. They reported that "most geologists and most of the
oil companies were convinced that there was no oil in Caldwell
County." Of the same import had been an article in the historical edition of the Lockhart *Post-Register* for August 3,
1936, in which the only reference to geology was the statement
that Davis had begun his seventh, and first successful, well
against the advice of his geologist. There was no reference to
the origin of the search for oil.

This search was quite typical of the times in that it was
initiated by local men motivated at least in part by the desire to
add a new resource to the not overly prosperous agricultural
economy. Two lawyers, Norman Dodge and Carl C. Wade,
asked a geologist, Verne Woolsey, to look for a place to drill.
Woolsey remarked that they were sitting on a fault at the
moment. He located the fault plane, and Dodge and Wade took
leases. Wade then went East seeking capital to drill.[31] He
succeeded in interesting Oscar Davis, who took stock amount-
ing to $75,000 in the newly organized Texas Southern Oil and
Lease Syndicate, and asked his brother Edgar to manage his
interests for a third of the profits. When the capital of the
syndicate was exhausted, Edgar Davis paid off the stock-
holders, including his brother, and organized the North and
South Oil Company to continue exploration.

He had been so confident of success that he had begun
three wells. After a total of six dry holes which used up the
fortune of a million and a half dollars he had made in rubber
plantations, he made, against the advice of his geologist, a location on the Raphael Rios property. The well came in August 8,
1922, and led to further development in Caldwell and Hays
counties.

In making this location Davis said he was guided by a deep faith in divine providence, and it was to divine guidance and not to geology that he ever afterward attributed his success. The preamble to the charter of the Luling Foundation (it is significant that it was not called the Edgar B. Davis Foundation) begins:

Believing that a kind and gracious Providence, who guides the Destinies of all humanity, directed me in the search for and the discovery of oil, and in our successful management and favorable outcome of the business, and believing that the wealth which has resulted has not come through any virtue or ability of mine, and desiring to discharge in some measure the trust which has been reposed in me; and in a spirit of gratitude to the Giver of all good for his beneficience....[32]

So successful was he in giving his money away that, although the state of Massachusetts secured a judgment, its representatives could find no assets to attach. The people of Caldwell and Hays counties resented the attempted raid by a Yankee state. Not all of them shared Davis' piety, but whatever their views on divine providence, Davis was their hero.

A feature writer for the *New York Times,* in an article published July 5, 1931, eight months after C. M. Joiner had brought in the discovery well in East Texas, wrote, "Geologists and other prospectors for the big oil companies had gone over this territory looking for signs of oil and had pronounced it barren, or at best unfavorable for commercial development." The statement is not wholly accurate, but it is what a journalist would have heard who visited East Texas in 1931.

It is less misleading than one that appeared in the Joiner obituary in the *Dallas Morning News,* March 29, 1947:

C. M. (Dad) Joiner, 87, the Shakespeare-quoting wildcatter who sank a battered bit into history's greatest oil field will be buried Saturday morning at Hillcrest Mausoleum.

Flat broke at 65, Joiner sank the epoch shattering East Texas field's first well on a shoe string on land where geologists had already ruled there was no oil.

The reporter was merely restating what had long been a popular tradition.

Probing for oil in the five counties (Upshur, Gregg, Rusk, Smith, and Cherokee) in which the East Texas pool lies began as early as 1901. Among the men who drilled was A. P. Boynton, who put down three wells, one of them only six miles from the pool Joiner was to discover.[33] Further interest was stimulated by the Mexia discovery in 1921. In that year J. A. Colliton drilled five wells in Cherokee County, having in the latter part of his venture financial help from Colonel Humphreys, the discoverer of Mexia. In one of the wells he struck oil, but failed to obtain commercial production. He attempted to interest the major companies, and according to local tradition, was told by the representative of one of them that he would drink all the oil produced in Cherokee County.[34]

Whether this is true or not, the major companies did send their geologists into the region. They were looking for faults and salt domes, which they did not find, and most of the major companies withdrew. But the vote of no confidence was not unanimous. Two geologists, Julius Fohs and James H. Gardner, had in 1915 recommended drilling near Kilgore. Their client had interested a subsidiary of the Shell Company in the project. The president of the company, also a geologist, drilled a mile from the location recommended. In so doing he missed discovering the East Texas field.[35]

Mose Knebel, then geologist for the Humble Company, induced his company to take leases. He failed to persuade them to drill, but the leases gave Humble a considerable interest in the East Texas field. Albert E. Oldham, a geologist for the Amerada Corporation, recommended that his company take leases on a block eight miles wide and twenty miles long at a cost of $150,000. The management was unwilling to commit this sum. If it had, Amerada would have been the biggest producer in East Texas.[36]

Finally, there is the seldom-mentioned fact that Joiner

availed himself of geological advice, though the extent to
which he followed it is not clear. Joiner had been a client of
A. D. Lloyd in Oklahoma,[37] and after he acquired his East
Texas leases he postponed making a location until Lloyd,
then busy in New Mexico, could advise him. But because he
had to agree to drill on the Daisy Bradford farm in order
to obtain a lease on it, he set up his rig two miles from the
spot Lloyd had picked. Whether Lloyd approved this second
location is not clear. After the loss of two holes, it was necessary to move to a third location. Mrs. Bradford and the crew
moved the rig down hill, the path of least resistance. Even so,
a sill broke after they had gone about 250 feet, and there
drilling began on the Daisy Bradford No. 3. Lloyd did not
approve of this location. He left East Texas and did not return
until the oil sand had been reached. When the well came in,
he and Joiner posed for a picture, and he was quoted as saying,
"Boys, this is the fourth time Joiner has found pay sand upon
my recommendation, and we're not going to let it get away
from him this time."[38] Later he went before the Henderson
Chamber of Commerce and pleaded with Joiner's creditors to
refrain from filing suits and to give the discoverer time to
develop his properties.

There was then a minority report on East Texas. The drill
proved that the majority was wrong, and "Remember East
Texas" became among geologists a warning against dogmatic
inflexibility. But the companies that had been misadvised
did not fire their geologists. The skeptics had already been
converted.

J. C. Donnell of the Ohio Oil Company had once said,
"When geology comes into the oil industry, I go out." Yet
within a few years his own company's geology department
was regarded as its most important division.[39] The Gulf Oil
Corporation in 1911 hired M. J. Munn away from the United
States Geological Survey and directed him to organize a geological staff.[40] By 1920 all but one or two of the large companies

had followed suit. The recovery of geology had been impressive. It had led to the finding of three-fourths of the oil discovered from 1920 to 1929.[41] During the next decade the refinement of geophysical instruments would give geologists and geophysicists new methods of exploring subsurface geology and further increase their chances of finding oil. Half the new reserves discovered from 1930 to 1959 were found by the use of the reflection seismograph.[42] Yet no instrument can find oil directly. Oil is still where you find it, and the only infallible geologist is, as John Galey said sixty years ago, Dr. Drill.

1. Samuel W. Tait, *The Wildcatters* (Princeton, 1946), p. 148. More recent writers, for example Carl Coke Rister, *Oil! Titan of the Southwest* (Norman, 1949) and Ruth Sheldon Knowles, *The Greatest Gamblers* (New York, 1959), do give considerable attention to geology.

2. M. G. Cheney, interview, April 4, 1942.

3. Charles N. Gould, *Covered Wagon Geologist* (Norman, 1959), p. 118.

4. A. I. Levorsen, *Geology of Petroleum* (San Francisco, 1956), p. 140; Knowles, *op. cit.*, pp. 72, 73.

5. Allen Hamill, tape-recorded interview, September 2, 1952.

6. Ed Prather, tape-recorded interview, April 4, 1954.

7. Benjamin Coyle, tape-recorded interviews, July 28 and 30, 1953.

8. Gould, *op cit.*, p. 178.

9. Lew Allen, "Oil Wildcatters," *New York Times* (July 30, 1922), VII, 3.

10. Boyce House, *Oil Boom* (Caldwell, Idaho, 1941), p. 141.

11. Sidney Paige, tape-recorded interview, June 7, 1954.

12. W. H. Bryant, tape-recorded interview, July 29, 1952.

13. Levorsen, *op. cit.*, p. 14.

14. On the early history of petroleum geology see J. V. Howell, "Historical Development of the Structural Theory of Accumulation of Oil and Gas," in *Problems of Petroleum Geology*, Sidney Powers Memorial Volume, edited by W. E. Wrather and F. H. Lahee, American Association of Petroleum Geologists (Tulsa, 1934), pp. 1-23; Ralph Arnold, "Two Decades of Petroleum Geology, 1902-1922," *Bulletin of the American Association of Petroleum Geologists*, VII (1923); Levorsen, *op. cit.*, pp. 138-41; Gould, *op. cit.*; Knowles, *op. cit.*

15. Levorsen, *op. cit.*, p. 140; Knowles, *op. cit.*, p. 73.

16. E. I. Thompson, tape-recorded interview, September 3, 1952.

17. Knowles, *op. cit.*, p. 153.

18. J. T. Young, tape-recorded interview, August 15, 1952.

19. Knowles, *op cit.*, pp. 181-82.

20. C. A. Warner, *Texas Oil and Gas Since 1954* (Houston, 1939), pp. 355, 375.

21. *Ibid.*, p. 19.

22. Patillo Higgins, tape-recorded interview, July 25, 1952.

23. Kenneth W. Porter to M.C.B., July 27, 1949.

24. James A. Clark and Michel Halbouty, *Spindletop* (New York, 1952), pp. 21-22.

25. *Ibid.*, pp. 24-26; House, *op cit.*, p. 23.

26. Knowles, *op. cit.*, p. 28; Clark and Halbouty, *op. cit.*, pp. 36-37.

27. Knowles, *op. cit.*, p. 29; Clark and Halbouty, *op cit.*, pp. 37-38; Rister, *op. cit.*, p. 53; Warner, *op. cit.*, p. 35.

28. Henrietta M. Larson and Kenneth W. Porter, *History of the Humble Oil and Refining Company* (New York, 1959), p. 16.

29. Stanley Walker, "Where Are They Now? Mr. Davis and His Millions," *New Yorker*, XXV (November 26, 1949), 35-47.

30. *Ibid.*

31. David Donogue, interview notes, 1947; Rister, *op. cit.*, pp. 174-77.

32. Lockhart *Post-Register*, August 3, 1936.

33. Henderson *Daily News*, November 30, 1938; Dorman H. Winfrey, "A History of Rusk County" (Master's thesis, University of Texas, 1951), p. 145.

34. Hattie Roach, *A History of Cherokee County* (Dallas, 1934), p. 80.

35. Rister, *op. cit.*, p. 366; Knowles, *op. cit.*, p. 267.

36. Knowles, *op. cit.*, p. 268; Larson and Porter, *op. cit.*, p. 397.

37. Rister, *op. cit.*, pp. 327-29; Knowles, *op. cit.*, p. 252; Harry Harter, *East Texas Oil Parade* (San Antonio, 1934), p. 41; Henderson *Daily News*, October 3, 1930.

38. Henderson *Daily Times,* September 23, 1930.

39. Arnold, *op. cit.*, p. 614.

40. Knowles, *op. cit.*, p. 146; Rister, *op. cit.*, p. 193.

41. Knowles, *op. cit.*, p. 240.

42. *Ibid.*, p. 280.

From Flygap to Whybark:
Some Unusual Texas Place Names

JOHN Q. ANDERSON

SUCH PROVOCATIVE place names as *Coonskin, Toadsuck, Why-bark, Flygap, Rollover,* and *Cream Level* are characteristic of a large number of unusual names that early settlers gave to villages, towns, and post offices in Texas.[1] Many of these names were ephemeral, as they were designations of post offices that were maintained briefly in a settler's home or in a store that moved when trails and roads changed or when the railroad came through. Other names of places that never achieved the importance of being post offices survived several years but were replaced by names of more favorable connotation. A few that are amusing to twentieth-century ears remained, such as *Bigfoot, Okra, Noodle,* and *Oatmeal.*

Strange as these early names seem to contemporary Texans, they are generally characteristic of the process of giving place names. As George R. Stewart has pointed out,[2] names given places during exploration and settlement of an area are usually transitory and descriptive, either of geographic features or of incidents involving the pioneers. Even so, Texas appears to have a very large number of unusual descriptive names, many of them facetious and ironical; consequently, they are of significance in the study of the folkways of early Texans. These names might be grouped in the following categories: descriptive names changed to more dignified designations;

euphemistic names; facetious and ironical names; and, finally, miscellaneous unusual names.[3]

I

Changes from the pungent and realistic names given many Texas villages and post offices to more respectable designations follow a pattern: first, as a camping place for hunters or renegades, some places acquired such derogatory names as *Hidetown* or *Thief Neck*. Then, when settlers arrived and established a community, such a name was unsuited for a prospective county seat, perhaps a future city. Thus, the petition for a post office submitted such dignified names as those of a substantial local citizen (perhaps the prospective postmaster), a town in an older state or foreign country, or a prominent terrain feature. This general process of naming was repeated numerous times in Texas between the 1820's and the 1920's. The pattern was interrupted by the Civil War and in several instances by Indian depredations which depopulated some border counties during that period. Furthermore, after the war, as railroad networks spread over the state, bypassed towns moved to the railroad and sometimes changed their names; and established names were displaced by those of railroad officials, their wives, daughters, and friends and by those of construction engineers and land promoters or townsite donors. Again, the discovery of oil in various parts of the state created a boom-and-bust atmosphere that brought towns into existence overnight and capriciously left others deserted; thus, the cycle was repeated in many instances long after the pioneer period had ended.

Of chief interest here are the changes from early names that indicate a closeness to the soil to later ones that are less realistically descriptive. For example, *Bear Hill*, Harris County, doubtless accurately named originally, became *Addicks* (1884)[4] for the first postmaster, and *Backbone Valley* (1874), Burnet County, was changed to *King Spring* in 1877. *Beaver Valley*,

Anderson County, became *Montalba* (1883) supposedly because someone noticed a snow-covered hill and fabricated a name from Latin.[5] *Bloody Hollow,* Delta County, became *Tranquil,*[6] suitable in 1961 for the site of a pill factory. J. Frank Dobie says that *Blackjack Grove,* Hopkins County, got its name from the favorite tune of a frontier fiddler; the name was later shortened to *Blackjack* and then changed to *Cumby*[7] for Bob Cumby, Confederate colonel. Also, Mr. Dobie tells this story about the naming of *Blessing,* Matagorda County: John Pierce was asked his opinion of having the St. Louis and Brownsville Railway cross his ranch and build a station and shipping pen; "Thank God!" he said and added, "It would be a blessing"; he proposed *Thank God* as the name of the station, but railroad officials who considered that irreverent accepted *Blessing.*[8]

Bucksnort is meaningless to contemporary Texans, but frontiersmen knew that it referred to the peculiar whistle or snort common to buck deer. There were three *Bucksnorts* in Texas. *Bucksnort,* Shelby County, changed to *Timpson* (1885), *Buck Snort* in Marion County became *Buena Vista,* and *Bucksnort* at the Falls of the Brazos in Falls County gave way to *Marlin* (1851).[9]

West Texas counties were the last to be affected by Victorian propriety: *Bull Head* (1879), Edwards County, was changed to *Vance* in 1886, and *Bull Valley,* Young County, became *Hawkins Chapel* for J. F. and S. J. Hawkins. When the Santa Fe Railroad was building across the XIT Ranch, the newly imported Hereford bulls insisted on lying on the track at a switch and causing the railroad men no end of trouble. As a result, the conductor referred to the switch as *Bull Town.* "But this was too vulgar for railroad men in the office," Mr. Dobie says, "and in making a map they changed it to Bovina."[10]

Pioneer Texas farmers who labored clearing the land, grubbing stumps, and working with an eye out for Indians

were naturally suspicious of those who did not work so hard—
storekeepers, for instance. That distrust may be the reason
behind *Cream Level* (1857), Parker County, which was
changed to *Veal's Station* within the year. *Creamlevel* (1888),
Van Zandt County, lasted three years, and *Cream* (1879),
Parker County, endured but one year. In Stephens County a
storekeeper named Spicer, evidently not an aggressive mer-
chandiser, replied to most inquiries for items that he was
"slap out"; in time the place came to be called *Slapout*.[11]
Bill Frank operated a store on Mukewater Creek on the
Jinglebob cattle trail in Coleman County. Like many other
men of the time, he was inordinately fond of practical jokes.
A favorite of his was to fill whiskey bottles with colored
water, set them alongside the bottles of whiskey, and sell them
to cowboys. When a name for the newly granted post office
was to be selected, the cowboys got their revenge by sending
in the name *Trick 'Em*, which the Post Office Department
changed to *Trickham* (1879).[12] Bruce Gray, Anderson County
storekeeper, had been unable to decide on a name for his
prospective post office; while filling a customer's bill of goods,
he noticed a request for a yard of cloth. And so he named his
post office *Yard* (1903).[13]

Despite the continued popularity of Davy Crockett, *Coonskin,* the first post office in San Jacinto County (1847), was
no name for a county seat. The name was changed for unknown
reasons to *Fireman's Hill* (1867) and three years later to
Cold Spring (two words), and finally to *Coldspring* (one
word), for springs in the area.[14] For a long time *Dog Town*
(1871) was the county seat of McMullen County. Cattlemen
in the area kept packs of dogs to hunt wild cattle, and dogs
outnumbered the people in the town ten to one. After the
presidential election of 1876, the town was called *Tilden,*
although locally it was still called *Dog Town*.[15]

The first name of *Blaconia* (1888), Bee County, was *Dark
Corner,* a derogatory term indicating a backward place, later

synonymous with "a wide place in the road" or "a tank town."[16] Even more revealing was *Discord* (1889), Coleman County, which was changed in 1890 to *Rockwood,* and *Gossip* (1888), Johnson County, which within the year was changed to *Venus.* A modern Texas metropolis with the name *Eli* is unimaginable. First called *Twin Buttes* for hills in Hall County, the name was changed to *Eli* in 1906 when a post office was granted; fires and a cyclone destroyed the town. It was rebuilt west of the old site and the post office was discontinued in 1914. When it was re-established in 1915, *Eli* became *Elite.*[17]

The occupation of buffalo hunting gave several pungent names to Texas places. For instance, *Hide Bug,* honoring the insect that ruined piles of buffalo hides left out in the weather, was the first name of present *White Star,* Motley County.[18] When buffalo hunters swarmed into the Panhandle, the last stronghold of the buffalo, a hunters' camp named *Hidetown* sprang up on Sweetwater Creek, Wheeler County. So notorious was the place that the army in 1876 located Fort Elliott some distance away to escape contamination. Later, when settlers arrived, *Hidetown* became *Mobeetie* (1879), supposedly an Indian word for either "walnut trees" or "sweet water."[19] *Hide Town,* too, was the name of *Snyder* (1883), Scurry County, when it was a supply camp for buffalo hunters; but, as Mr. Dobie says, "When the smell of buffalo hides was no longer noticeable, the people sniffed and called their town Snyder."[20] Much earlier, in the days of the Republic, *Halletts-ville* (1849), Lavaca County, had been called *Hidesville* for the buffalo hides brought there; it was also called *Hicksville,* not facetiously but for A. W. Hicks who owned a hotel there in 1846.[21] One town in Texas still exists which recalls hides— cowhides, not buffalo. During the Republic cattle in South Texas were so numerous that they were killed for the hides, which were more valuable than the meat. Mr. Dobie says, "On a creek in DeWitt County cattle that bogged, or perhaps were cunningly killed near the bog holes so that their carcasses would not arouse suspicion, furnished so many hides that the stream acquired the name of Cuero (Hide). The town of Cuero took its name from this creek."[22] But, of course, the Spanish *Cuero* (1846) did not have the same connotation for Anglo ears.

The frontier staple foods hog meat and corn were responsible for several early names. The first name of *Plano* (1852), Collin County, was *Hominyville*, changed to what Dr. Henry Dye surmised was the Spanish word for plain.[23] At least six places had the distinction of being called *Hogeye*. Mr. Dobie tells of a settlement near the line between Jack and Wise counties in which a doctor named Shelton and a cowman named Earhart each wished the prospective town named for him. The community divided into factions. The Shelton side won, but the ranch people dubbed the place *Hogeye*. Mr. Dobie also mentions a *Hog Eye* (1902) in Gregg County and one in Caldwell County. Before the Civil War a strolling fiddler stopped at the Lytton home, near *Lytton Springs* (1888), and the whole community gathered for a dance. The fiddler could play only one tune, a piece called "Hog Eye." Because he played it all night, the term became a byword in the community and fastened itself to the Lytton home.[24] It may have been that same fiddler who caused a place in adjoining Bastrop County to be called *Hogeye*. Originally called *Glasscock*, it was renamed *Hogeye* for the favorite tune of a Negro fiddler but was later changed to *Elgin* (1873) to honor Robert Morris Elgin, land commissioner, who laid out the site of the town. Also, the first store at the site of St. Elmo, Sterling County, was called both *Hogeye* and *Wildhog*.[25] Whether a fiddle tune or the expression "in a pig's eye" (as Mr. Dobie suggests) is the reason for the popularity of the name *Hogeye*, the one in Hunt County acquired the name in a peculiar way. M. Walworth Harrison wrote in 1961 that the eye in the emblem on the Masonic Lodge in Mount Carmel looked like a hog's eye to the natives, and so they called the place *Hog Eye*.

The same "coonskin" phraseology caused *Lick Skillet* to be applied to at least six different places in Texas. The expression might mean a scarcity of food or "too little and too late." "In pioneer days nearly all meat was fried in a skillet," Mr. Dobie explains; "then gravy, well thickened with flour burned brown, was made of the grease. A boy might sop the skillet with a biscuit or a hound might lick it."[26] According to Rea A. Nunnallee of Van Alstyne, when *Pilot Grove*, Grayson County, was only a stage stop, the cooking was so good that the passengers "licked the skillet clean," and so the place was called *Lick Skillet*."[27] *Fayette*, Fayette County, came by the name because its public barbecues attracted so many people that on one occasion late-comers found little food and were told that they would have to "lick the skillets." In revenge they dubbed the town *Lick Skillet*.[28] M. H. Marwil of Henderson says that *Lick Skillet* was an early name of *Harmony Hill* (1854), Rusk County. In addition, a rural community in Leon County and a Negro community in Milam County were both called *Lick Skillet*.[29]

Similarly, *Nip and Tuck*, a colloquialism from horse racing, designated at least three places. In Leon County a spring that furnished water for settlers was overrun in summer when people rushed there early in the morning. "It was nip and tuck," one man said, "as to who got there first."[30] *Nip-and-Tuck* in Rusk County was another derisive name for *Harmony Hill*.[31] The first saloon in *Big Spring*, Howard County, run by George Bauer and Cal Williams, was called *Nip and Tuck*, perhaps for the same reason for which a community in Northeast Louisiana about the same time was given the same name. Of this place it was said that it was "nip and tuck" whether the settlers would survive.[32]

One of the most extreme examples of change from a "coonskin" name to an elegant one is *Pinhook*, Lamar County, which became *Paris*. According to Daniel F. Latimer, *Pinhook*, which began as a store in 1837, got its name from his cousin

who, when told that Daniel and his brother fished in Baker
Branch with bent pins for hooks, replied that it was just a
"pin hook sort of a place."[33] There is, by the way, still a
Pinhook in Lamar County. Another extreme change was in
the name of *Poor* (1888), Leon County, which became
Wealthy (1894). Evidently this was the work of Jesse P. Quinn,
postmaster at the time. *Possum Trot* and *Punkin Center* appear
to be twentieth-century fabrications. However, *Fullbright*,
Red River County, was called *Possum Trot* about 1850. Near
the present *Cottage Hill*, Collin County, was a school which
before 1854 was quite logically called *Possum Trot* because
possums in great numbers fed on the red and black haws and
persimmons on Haw Branch.[34]

When Abe Winkle opened a store in Lamb County in
1928, he called it *Punkin Center*, but when the highway was
built circling the town the name was changed to *Circle*. On
the other hand, there is still a *Punkin Center* in Dawson
County. *Pumpkinville*, one of the early names of *Tivydale*,
Gillespie County, was also called *Bunkesville* for a local group
of German-American musicians who organized the Bunkesville
Band and played old-time German tunes. *Poverty Flat* was
the name cowboys gave to a settlement of nesters in Childress
County in the belief that they could not survive; but survive
they did, and according to Mr. Dobie the Post Office Department assigned their post office the "characterless" name *Tell*.
A local historian explains that the community was originally
called *Lee* (1888) but was changed to *Tell Tale Flat* because
people revealed too much unsolicited information to the grand
jury (presumably about fraudulent land claims). The Post
Office Department shortened the name to *Tell* (1905).[35]

Paluxy, Hood County, had a difficult time arriving at a
suitable name. First called *Pull Tight* because a sand hill near
by required teams of horses and mules to "pull tight" to get up
it, it was successively called *Pull Tight, Goather's, Himmons
and Haley's Mill, Poloxeyville, Polexyville, Paluxieville,* and

finally *Paluxy* (1873), which may or may not be a corruption of *Biloxi* (probably for Biloxi, Mississippi).[36] The town of *Skin Tight,* Cherokee County, retained that name from its founding until it was granted a post office and took the patriotic name of *Lone Star* (1883). *Pinehill* (1847), Rusk County, was called *Rake Pocket* for a long time after a traveler was robbed in a hostelry in the village.[37] The reverse of that situation is *Fair Play* (1851), Panola County, settled by John Allison, who had a general store, a boarding-house, and a blacksmith shop and who was county judge when the county was organized. A traveler, impressed with the fair rates and treatment he received at Allison's place, gave it the name *Fair Play;* one account says the traveler was Sam Houston.[38]

Appearances sometimes gave names that could not last. Five places in Texas were once called *Ragtown.* Two of them were rural communities in Lamar and Shelby counties, and their names doubtless reflect the difficulties of pioneer years. This may also have been the case with *Ragtown,* Castro County, which became *Cleo* (1902). However, *Post* (1907), Garza County, a town which from its inception had the fortune of cereals millionaire C. W. Post behind it, could hardly have been poor; yet it was called *Ragtown* because residents lived in tents on the bare prairie until they could build the model city to please Mr. Post.[39] Another tent city called *Ragtown* was built in anticipation of the arrival of the railroad; the name was changed to *Rotando* with the granting of a post office in 1906 and again changed to *Rotan,* Fisher County, the same year.[40] At the other end of the state, *Rollover* (1897), Galveston County, recalled the early times when pirates "rolled over" their contraband across the narrowest part of Bolivar Peninsula from the Gulf to the Bay. That wonderfully descriptive name was changed to *Caplen* in 1907. Similarly, *Saddle Creek,* McCulloch County, seemed unsuitable to J. E. White, who had a store there and who got a post office in the name of *Pear Valley* (1910).[41]

Section Four was the name of a town in Montgomery County, a name it took somehow from the Houston, East and West Texas Railroad. Because of the initials H.E.W.T., local citizens called the narrow-gauge railroad "Hell Either Way You Take It" or the "Cottontail Limited" because, just like a rabbit, it stopped behind every stump. *Section Four* became *Splendora* when C. C. Cox obtained a post office in 1896, and a plaque on the site says it was named "for the splendor of its surroundings."[42] During the Civil War and Reconstruction period, *Carpenter's Bluff*, Grayson County, was called *Thief Neck* because the saloon in the general store was a rendezvous for notorious characters.

A few other changes for status: *Spanky*, Navarro County, became *Dresden* (1852); *Truebsal*, Fayette County, was facetiously called *Trouble* until changed to *Winedale; Sand Fly* (1853), Bastrop County, was changed in 1869 to *Pontotoc; Tickey* (1888), Collin County, became *Viney* in 1890; *Twist* (1899), Swisher County, changed to *Auburn* in 1910; *Wayback* (1844), Coryell County, became *Pearl* (1890). And, finally, *Toadsuck*, Grayson County, doubtless for good reason, was changed to *Collinsville* (1872).

Of course, many other towns and post offices with more ordinary names to begin with changed their names to flatter politicians, generous citizens, railroad officials, or a new postmaster, but most of the unusual ones cited here changed because the people felt that early "coonskin" names were not indicative of the substantial communities they hoped to build.

II

Numerous other villages and post offices started with euphemistic names designed to launch them under favorable auspices. Most of these names were also transitory, despite their pretentiousness. Such names need no explanation, but their number reflects the late nineteenth-century optimism that prevailed at the time when most of them were given.

Name	County	Post Office Established
Acme (3)	Hockley	1887
	Van Zandt	1891
	Hardeman	1898
Advance	Parker	1894
Alert	Hardin	1901
Ample	Haskell	1890
Apex	San Saba	1880
Bonanza	Hopkins	1898
Balm	Cooke	1889
Bonami	Jasper	1902
Boom	Castro	1903
Busyton	Hamilton	1880
Charity (2)	Polk	1896
	Parker	1880
Climax (2)	Collin	1895
	Nacogdoches	none
Content (3)	Runnels	1882
	Coleman	1909
	Colorado	1865
Dawn	Deaf Smith	1889
Dreamland	Starr	none
Eclipse	Gaines	1904
Eden	Nacogdoches	none
Eldorado	Schleicher	1895
Elysian Fields	Harrison	1848
Elysium	Bastrop	1896
Energy	Comanche	1897
Enterprise	Medina	1890
Equality	Harrison	1882
Eulogy	Bosque	1887
Eureka (2)	Kaufman	1857
	Navarro	1886
Experiment	Galveston	1860
Fairyland	Hopkins	1880
Forward	Lamar	1904
Friendship	Harrison	1851
Freedom	Harris	1855
Gleam	Lee	1889
Glory	Lamar	1881
Good Luck	Uvalde	1879
Gratis	Orange	1910
Happy	Swisher	1891
Happy Hollow	Burnet	1876

NAME	COUNTY	POST OFFICE ESTABLISHED
Happy Land	Nolan	1886
Harmony	Nacogdoches	1911
Help	Bosque	1894
Honest	Delta	1897
Hope	Lavaca	1857
Hopewell	Smith	1887
Ideal	Sherman	1907
Lucky	Montague	1902
Mecca	Madison	1894
Mount Enterprise	Rusk	1866
New Hope	Dallas	1886
Nobility	Fannin	1881
Okay	Bell	1896
Omen	Smith	1892
Paradise	Wise	1890
Peaceville	Hutchinson	1905
Placid	McCulloch	1908
Plenitude	Anderson	1850
Pluck	Polk	1918
Pride	Dawson	1904
Progress (3)	Hale	1892
	Hidalgo	1900
	Bailey	1927
Progreso	Hidalgo	1930
Prospect (2)	Clay	1893
	McLennan	1890
Prosper	Collin	1893
Prosperity	Falls	1853
Providence	Van Zandt	1888
Rest	Caldwell	1880
Saluria	Matagorda	1848
Seclusion	Lavaca	1879
Security	Montgomery	1910
Solitude (2)	Brazoria	1849
	El Paso	1903
Sublime	Lavaca	1875
Superior	Brazoria	1894
Thrift	Wichita	1925
Thrifty	Brown	1880
True	Young	1894
Utopia	Uvalde	1885
Veribest	Tom Green	1926
Welfare	Kendall	1889

NAME	COUNTY	POST OFFICE ESTABLISHED
Wonders	Nacogdoches	1871
Worthy	Uvalde	1907
Zenith	Swisher	1892

Omitted from this list are a number of euphemistic-descriptive names, such as *Fairview* and *Golden Vale,* and family names, such as *Joy, Jolly,* and *Best.* Probably a whole group of names centering around *sun* and *star* should have been included. A few of these are: *Sunbeam* (1890), Grayson County; *Sunny Lane* (1881), Burnet County; *Sunshine* (1884), Houston County; and *Rising Star,* one in Shackelford County in 1882 and one in Eastland County in 1883.

Amusing as these unblushingly optimistic names may seem to suburbanites, they are no more pretentious than the euphemistic names real estate promoters have given to suburbs in every Texas town and city, such as Crestwood, Bellaire, Highland Park, River Oaks, Ravenwood, Tanglewood, and Culpepper Manor. Most of the nineteenth-century namers were more honest than the promoters of the Rio Grande Valley back in the 1920's who produced such monstrosities as *San Perlita* (for someone named Pearl), *La Pryor* (for a promoter named Pryor), and *La Sara* (for the wives of two promoters).

III

Concurrent with the desire to achieve dignity and a propitious beginning through names existed a counterimpulse of humor and fantasy in early Texans. It was the same spirit that produced the practical joke, the tall tale, the anecdote, and the masculine fun of the "Big Bear School" of American humor. Settlers in Texas, faced with shortages of all kinds, Indians, violent weather, and impossible distances, were sometimes more impressed with contemporary reality than with future potential and thus gave facetious and ironical names to places and post offices. Similarly, they sometimes looked at themselves and their foibles with astonishing clarity and named accordingly.

The result was a large number of amusing names, for some of which there are traditional explanations; for others there are none.

The severity of Texas weather is evident in *Arctic*, Jack County, which became a post office on December 20, 1880, during the "blue norther" season. *Freezeout* was the original name of *Sandow*, Milam County, and *Polar* (1906), Kent County, doubtless came from the same circumstances. When a group of surveyors in Brown County in the 1870's were caught in a norther on the Plains, they facetiously named a town *Zephyr*. Ironically, *Zephyr* (1888) was destroyed by a tornado in 1903. It was rebuilt, however, and still exists. *Cold Hill* (1883) may recall someone's winter camp. At the other extreme is *Hot* (1897), Shelby County. *Sprinkle* (1885), Travis County, might have referred to lack of rain or to a form of baptism, but the reference of *Mud* (1887), also in Travis County, is quite certain. *Desert* (1893), Collin County, was doubtless established in a drought year. *Duster* (1890), Comanche County, supposedly got its name when, at a meeting of citizens to pick a name, a man picked up a piece of paper on which a dust storm had deposited a film of earth; he shook off the dirt and wrote the word "duster."[43] The same type of weather doubtless gave the name *Grit* (1901), Mason County, although later stories state that the name honors the perseverance of early settlers. There was also a *Grit* (1897) in Medina County.

Since most settlers in West Texas were farmers, the name *Blowout* (1875), Llano County, recalled that heartbreaking situation in which wind-driven sand in the spring seared new crops in the field. "Nubbin" in pioneer times usually meant an ear of corn undeveloped as a result of drought; or it might indicate a child that was small for its age. The ridge between Keechi and Boggy creeks in Leon County was first called *Pleasant Ridge* but was then renamed *Nubbin Ridge* (1877) when the land proved to be poor.

Those pioneer namers who looked at what they had instead

of what they might have indicated the results in names. A post office in Stephens County in 1893 was called *Necessity*, and one in Lamar County, *Need* (1888). *Needmore*, Bailey County, was jokingly so called by a townsite optimist who said that they needed more settlers. A Delta County community, settled during the Republic, was called *Pecan* (1873) but was changed to *Needmore* in 1886. *Needmore* was the name of a rural school in Nacogdoches County. When August Schendel built a store in Fort Bend County in the 1890's, he called it *Schendelville*, but when the post office was applied for, *Needmore* was suggested as a joke, supposedly because "life then was so hard on the prairie farms and the returns uncertain and small." The Post Office Department named it *Needville* (1894).[44] *Needmore* was the nickname of what became *Pine Town*, Cherokee County, because the one store at the location was considered insufficient. The place had already had a more interesting change of name: for a time it was called *Java* because a young lady at a dance lost a petticoat on which the letters still plainly showed that the garment had been made from a Java coffee sack. The post office, established while that story was current, was named *Java* (1895).[45] Though never a town or post office, *Needmore Creek* in Hemphill County in the Panhandle got its name, according to John Isaacs, because two cowboys who ran a supply store at the mouth of the creek often ran short of supplies and consistently wrote, "We need more bacon, potatoes, etc."[46] Two other amateur storekeepers in Coleman County named their store and post office *Novice* (1885) to indicate their lack of experience; wags said it meant "no vice." They were more certain than a man named Kerchain in Falls County who applied for a post office but submitted no name; when the Post Office Department chided him for not suggesting a name, he reportedly said, "I'm just a stranger in the place," and the name became *Stranger* (1879).[47] Though *Slocum* (1898), Anderson County, appears to be a family name, the story is that E. T. McDaniel worked very hard to get a post office and even carried the mail six months without pay. When his request was finally granted and he was installed as postmaster in his store, he named the place *Slocum* because the post office had been, he said, "a *slow come*."[48] Such puns were enjoyed by early Texans. For example, *Cash* (1895), Hunt County, had as its first postmaster John A. Money, and *Chancey* (1890), Bowie County, had Benjah Chance.

Some early post office names show a love for the fantastic, fanciful, and whimsical. Dallas County had a post office named *Buck and Breck* (1857), perhaps the given names of two men, and *Bug Eye* (1872). *Bug Tussle*, Fannin County, has been publicized by Frank X. Tolbert of the *Dallas Morning News*,[49] but there was a *Big Tussel* in Leon County, an early name for *Flynn*. The name of Bell County, which has both *Belton* (Bell-town) and *Belfalls*, tempted someone to come up with *Ding Dong*, which is still on State Highway Department maps. *Drop* was a post office in Denton County from 1886 to 1905, and *Dump* was the name of two post offices, one in Collin County from 1899 to 1904 and one in Limestone County for about a year (1888). *Dull*, LaSalle County, was established as the Dulls Ranch post office in 1889, and *Big Lump*, Milam County, existed from 1912 to 1924.

Longneck, Collin County,[50] probably indicated a formation of land, but *Roughneck* (1884), Blanco County, seems to ante-date oil-field terminology. M. Walworth Harrison of Green-ville says that Hunt County had communities called *Goose Neck, Stump Toe*, and *Sweat Box*.[51] *Lost* (1900), Matagorda County, doubtless referred to location rather than residents; significantly Post Office Department records show the post office "never in operation." *Mirage*, a post office in Deaf Smith County, lasted from 1891 to 1895.

Oatmeal, Burnet County, was established as a post office in 1853, and the same name still appears on State Highway Department maps. *Pancake* was a post office in Coryell County between 1884 and 1886, and then *Bush* (1894) in the same county changed to *Pancake*. The obvious explanation is not food but the postmaster—John M. N. Pancake. *Pone* (1898) Rusk County, was short for *Short Pone*, supposedly because the people were accused of subsisting on "pone" bread. *Pone* still appears on maps, as does *Okra* (1899), Eastland County.

Human weaknesses and vanity gave names to several places. For example, *Ambia* (1887), Lamar County, was named by J. P. Minor of nearby Roxton, who said that he derived the word from "amber" because the men of the community were the greatest tobacco chewers and spitters he had ever seen. Lamar County residents' fondness for chewing tobacco was further attested by *Razor* (1904), which A. K. Haynes named for plug tobacco he sold in his store.[52] Some said that *Direct* (1887), also in Lamar County, was named because Indians from Indian Territory across Red River came there "direct" for whiskey; others, however, said that a revivalist so emphatically stated that local residents were going "straight to hell" that *Direct* seemed appropriate. *Saint Jo* (1873), Montague County, is not a transfer name from another state: a townsite at a place first called *Head of Elm* (1860-73) was being laid out by Irb H. Bogges and Joe A. Howells. As incentive, Bogges provided the volunteer surveying crew with a jug of whiskey; but Howells, a temperate man, was made ill by a single drink. Bogges remarked that "Old Joe" was so "saintly" they would call the new town *Saint Jo*.

Gambling, as well as whiskey and tobacco, gave names to places. *Concan* (1886), Uvalde County, Mr. Dobie says, got the name either from "coon can," a game that Negroes play with both dice and cards, or from the Mexican card game of *con quien* ("with whom"), derived from the Portuguese *con quian*.[53] *Fodice* (1902), Houston County, is said to be named for a favorite Negro gambling game called "Four Dice," or possibly to be a misspelling of Fordyce, Arkansas.

Fort Growl, Young County, will not be found on any military map or in post office records. During the Civil War, A. B.

Medlan fortified his house against the Indians, who were a far greater menace than the Yankees in that area, and the people gathered at his "fort" during Indian scares. "There were many dogs," he said, but, meaningfully, "they did not do all the growling."[54] *Barnardville,* Hood County, named for Charles Barnard, who had a store there, was a perfectly good name until several fights occurred in the vicinity. Signs suddenly appeared along the road showing the distance to "Fort Spunky," and so *Fort Spunky* became the post office in 1886 and the name still appears on county maps.[55] Perhaps *Scrap* (1903), Red River County, also resulted from rough-and-tumble fighting, and the *West Scrap* which shows on the Red River County map today may be a "suburb" of the original *Scrap.* Certainly *Scrapping Valley,* Jasper County, got its name from a fight; according to Judge V. O. Easley, at a singing school in 1910 a girl gave a boy her picture which he for some reason tore up. After singing was over, the girl thrashed him publicly. The story has a Hollywood ending; they got married.[56]

Licke was a post office in Fannin County between 1848 and 1861 and was followed by *Lick,* 1870-71; the name may have referred to a salt lick or possibly molasses, which was also called "lick" on the frontier. According to Winnie Brown, librarian in San Saba County, *Clabber Ridge* was the name of a place near the present *Locker* where camp meetings of two and three weeks' duration were held to which the campers brought their milk cows.[57] For *Flygap* (1884), Mason County, there is no immediate explanation. But *Tailholt,* a settlement of Tennessee mountaineers in Blanco County, explains itself.[58]

Some namers apparently had little faith in people. *Anti,* for instance, was the name of a post office in Cass County between 1888 and 1904. *Clip* (1898), Goliad County, lasted less than a year; *Cost,* Gonzales County, existed from 1897 to 1914. *Noodle* (1900), Jones County, was named for Noodle Creek near by. The name of the creek doubtless recalled some human foolishness, because "noodle" was once synonymous with "empty-headed." Could *Nutsford*, Lampasas County, a post office that lasted less than a year in 1887, have received its name for the same reason? *Looneyville* (1874), Nacogdoches County, may recall a family name rather than the condition of people in the community. Of darker implication are *Rat*, Burnet County, which existed on Post Office Department records only from June 2, 1880, to July 29, 1880, and *Sodom*, Hunt County, a post office from 1894 until 1901. *Muckymuck* (1886), Travis County, may have resulted from the fiddler's tune variously called "Monkey Mush" or "Money Much" or from the expression "high muckymuck," a scornful designation for a conceited person. *Naught*, Henderson County, changed to *Stockard* within the year 1899. A settlement along Lincoln Ridge, Collin County, was called *Squeezepenny*, doubtless by outsiders.[59] *Crackers Neck*, Chambers County, was recorded in 1860, which seems early for the now current nickname of Georgians. *Crush* (1899), Milam County, was named for its first postmaster, David P. Crush. *Exile* (1885), Uvalde County, a post office on the W. C. Lee ranch, was so called because it was so far from any settled area. In the negative vein also is *Notrees*, Ector County; in 1935 Charles Brown's request for a post office described the location as a treeless plain; the name was taken from his description.[60] The same conditions may explain *Noview* (1913), Dickens County. *Shy* was a post office in Madison County between 1902 and 1907. A schoolhouse near *Oxbow*, Hall County, where church and singing were held, was called *Squallin' Holler* by the cowboys who said if they could not sing they could squall and holler.[61] But what could be the explanation of *Straddle* (1880), Chambers County, and *Ketch Any*, a school in Collin County in 1860?

And these: *Purgatory Springs* (1890), Hays County; *Quicksand* (1871), Johnson County; *Snipe* (1921), Brazoria County; *Stump* (1892), Henderson County; *Tax* (1899), Leon County; *Veto*, two of them—Jack County, 1893, and Gillespie County,

1887; *Whybark* (1902), Bowie County; and *Yuno* (1892), Angelina County.

IV

A final group of unusual names of towns and post offices in early Texas defies any classification. Some of them recall everyday objects and occurrences, some refer to incidents long since forgotten, and some were merely pleasant to the ear.

That faithful servant of a motorless age, the horse, is remembered in several names, both as a draft animal and as a cow pony. *Dobbin* (1909), Montgomery County, was, of course, synonymous with the old, gentle work horse; the earlier name of the post office was *Bobbin* (1880). At the other extreme is the half-wild horse recalled in *Broncho* (so spelled in 1885), Tom Green County, and present *Bronco,* Yoakum County. Someone fancied up the horse by calling a post office in Johnson County *Equestria* (1883). Another kind of horse is indicated in *Race Track* (1888), Delta County, and *Trot* (1886), Polk County, although the latter may have been a shortening of *Possum Trot.*

In view of their prevalence at one time, it seems that there should have been more than the one *Cowboy* (1879), in McCulloch County. Cowboy equipment gave several names: *Ropesville* (1888), Nueces County, and *Ropesville* (1920), Hockley County; *Lariat* (1925), Parmer County; *Pack Saddle* (1888), Llano County; and *Horseshoe* (1888), Erath County. Related are *Stampede* (1893), Bell County, and *Rustler* (1905), Eastland County. Ranches are noted in *J Bob* (1879), Brown County, and *Hash Knife* (1879), Taylor County; of course, other towns named for ranches have survived, such as *Spur, Spade, Matador, Goodnight,* and *Loving.*

Early Texans did not want to remember Indians, but a few names point to them: *Lookout* (1893), Bexar County, and *Lookout* (1885), Leon County; and *Teepee* (1879), Motley County, probably for *Tee Pee Creek* which in turn noted an

Indian camping place. *Gunsight* (1880), Stephens County, says Mr. Dobie, was "so named either because an Indian shot the front sight off a gun with which a teamster was drawing a bead on him or because in the vicinity a hill and a gap between other hills line up like sights of a gun."[62]

The arrival of the machine age, automobiles, and oil shows in such post office names as *Auto* (1907), Howard County, and *Gasoline* (1907), Briscoe County, so named when a gasoline-operated gin was established. (It still appears on maps.) *Gusher* (1904), Hardin County, reflects the coming of oil. Much earlier was *Benzine* (1880), Jackson County. Then, there was *Turpentine* in Jasper County in 1926. Three names for modern gadgets —names that still survive—are: *Exray* (1897), Erath County, *Telephone* (1886), Fannin County, and *Telegraph* (1900), Kimble County.

"Culture" was missing from the Texas frontier; it could not even survive in names. *Poetry*, Kaufman County, lasted from 1880 to 1905; *Poet* (1898), Milam County, is shown as "never in operation"; and *Poet*, Dickens County, was changed to *Gilpin* within the year 1908. *Music*, Frio County (perhaps a family name?), lasted only part of the year 1880, and *Zither* (1900), Montgomery County, is marked "never in operation." *Violin* (1902), Hutchinson County, lasted somewhat longer.

Some people and incidents account for additional unusual names: *Bigfoot* (1883), Frio County, honors Bigfoot Wallace. *Friday* (1903), Trinity County, took its name from the postmaster, James F. Friday, as did *Noxville* (1879), Kimble County, from Persis Nox. *Baby Head* (1879), Llano County, recalls Comanche raids. *Dimple* (1901), Red River County, probably honored some pretty girl. *Cyclone* (1886), Bell County, was the old-fashioned name for tornado. *Iron Clad* (1867), Limestone County, doubtless referred to the "Iron Clad Oath" that defeated Confederates were supposed to take. One day Jack Cook and some men were in a plow shop in Lampasas County discussing the name for a new town. Cook noticed the brand name "Moline" on a plow, and so the place was named *Moline* (1910).[63] *Benonine* (1909), Wheeler County, supposedly got its name from a card game in which the winning hand would have been four nines, but one card was something else and the loser said, "It should have *been a nine!"*—which sounds like a story much after the fact. (There was a post office named *Nine* and one named *Four*.)

Adieu (1880), Jack County, must simply have sounded good to the namer, as perhaps did *Antiquity* (1880), Anderson County, not to mention the three *Echoes*—Bell County (1884), Jack County (1900), and Coleman County (1910). *Big Dollar* (1852), Wood County, could have been named for an oversized member of the Dollar family or the scarce coin on the frontier. *Cut* (1903), Henderson County, probably antedates its more famous counterpart, *Cut and Shoot*. *Democrat* (1893), Comanche County, complements *Voxpopuli* (1880), Colorado County. *Dew* (1885), Freestone County, could be a family name, but certainly *Dewdrop* (1895), Liberty County, is not. The *Wise* in Wise County produced *Owl* (1903). *Pink Hill* (1874), Grayson County, and *Pink* (1903), San Augustine County, would certainly be unsuitable names since the rise of communism.

Pointblank, San Jacinto County, established as a post office in 1884 and still flourishing, supposedly was named by Florence Dissiway, a French governess from Alabama. While tending the children of Henry and R. T. Robinson, she called the place *Blanc Point,* which later became *White Point,* then *Point Blank,* and finally *Pointblank*—a story after the fact?[64]

But no story has been discovered to explain *Pocket* (1897), Wharton County; *Rear* (1902), Red River County; *Sport* (1899), Aransas County; *Stop* (1901), San Augustine County; *Strip* (1904), Hale County; *Time* (1896), Sabine County; *Toto* (1894), Parker County; *Walk* (1888), Lampasas County; or *Zigzag* (1901), Medina County.

The stories of *Dime Box, Cut and Shoot,* and *Tarzan* are familiar from many tellings in newspapers.

For early Texans, arriving at a suitable place name was
often a difficult matter, like naming a new baby in a frontier
family that had already exhausted biblical names; the namer
might go, as he would put it, "from A to Izard." And that is
evidently what someone did in Coryell County in 1888 when
Izard became a post office. Or the process might lead to the
frustration experienced by the Travis County namer who in
1880 simply gave up and called his post office—*Nameless.*

1. No scientific study of Texas geographic and place names has
been made, as has been done in California, Arizona, and a few other
states. Geographical listing of names appears in Henry Gannett's *A
Gazetter of Texas* (Dept. of the Interior, U.S. Geological Survey, Bulletin
No. 224 [Washington, D.C., 1904]). Historical and traditional information about many Texas place names is included in *The Handbook of
Texas*, ed. Walter P. Webb (2 vols., Austin, 1952); J. Frank Dobie,
"Stories in Texas Names," *Southwest Review*, XXI (Winter, Spring, Summer, 1936), 125-36, 278-93, 411-17, and "Stories in Texas Place Names,"
in *Straight Texas* ("Publications of the Texas Folklore Society," XIII
[1937]), pp. 1-78; Z. T. Fulmore, *The History and Geography of Texas
as Told in County Names* (Austin, 1915); and Fred I. Massengill, *Texas
Towns: Origin of Names and Location of Each of the 2,148 Post Offices
in Texas* (Terrill, Texas, 1936). Information for this article is taken
largely from "Records of Appointments of Postmasters—Texas, 1846-1929,"
a microfilm copy of Records of the Post Office Department (National
Archives [Washington, 1960]), from county histories both in print and
as Masters' theses submitted to colleges in Texas, and from questionnaires
sent to county librarians and newspaper editors.

A grant from the Organized Research Fund, Texas A. and M. College, for parts of the summers of 1960 and 1961 has made this work
possible.

2. In his article on place names in the *Encyclopedia Britannica*,
Stewart sets up nine categories, all of which are illustrated by post office
names in Texas: descriptive (Elm Grove), incident (Duster), possessive
(Carroll's Prairie), commemorative and transfer (Snyder, Athens), euphe-
mistic (Good Luck, Paradise), manufactured (Tonola, Allamoore), shift
(Double Horn), and mistakes (Purdon, Tulia).

3. These categories are not "scientific" according to the rules of
onomatology, the emphasis here being historical and folkloristic.

4. Dates in parentheses after names are dates post offices were established; hyphenated dates, 1884-86, indicate duration of the post office.

Dates cited are from "Records of Appointments of Postmasters—Texas, 1846-1929" (microfilm), hereafter cited as R.A.P.

5. *The Handbook of Texas,* hereafter cited as H.B.T. Explanations that are not otherwise documented are from H.B.T.

6. Miss Sue Allbright, Law Library, Southern Methodist University, a native of Delta County.

7. *Op. cit.,* p. 287.

8. *Ibid.,* p. 281. R.A.P. shows that the first post office at that location was called Demings Bridge (1858), Edwin A. Deming, postmaster. The name was changed to Hawley in 1899 and to Blessing in 1903.

9. *Ibid.,* p. 292; Walter W. Brawn, "The History of Falls County" (Master's thesis, Baylor University, 1938), p. 30.

10. *Op. cit.,* pp. 290-91. Bovina, Parmer County, became a post office in 1899.

11. Mrs. H. F. Pearson, native of Stephens County, to J.Q.A., 1960.

12. Beatrice Grady Gay, *"Into the Setting Sun," A History of Coleman County* (privately printed, 1936), p. 17.

13. H.B.T.

14. Ruth Hansbro, "A History of San Jacinto County, 1870-1940" (Master's thesis, Sam Houston State College, 1940), pp. 19-20.

15. "Legends of 'Dog Town' Linger On," *Bryan Daily Eagle,* June 2, 1960.

16. Mrs. I. C. Madray, *A History of Bee County* (Beeville, Texas, 1939).

17. Inez Baker, *Yesterday in Hall County, Texas* (Memphis, Texas, 1940).

18. Harry H. Campbell, *The Early History of Motley County* (San Antonio, 1958).

19. Lula Mae Farley, "Young Swiss Finds Home," *Amarillo Sunday News and Globe,* Golden Anniversary Edition, 1938, Sec. C, p. 6.

20. Dobie, *op. cit.,* p. 289.

21. Paul C. Boethel, *Sand in Your Craw* (Austin, 1959), pp. 95-97.

22. Dobie, *op. cit.,* p. 133.

23. Harold Beam, "A History of Collin County, Texas" (Master's thesis, University of Texas, 1951), p. 86.

24. Dobie, *op. cit.,* pp. 285-86.

25. Ira L. Watkins, "The History of Sterling County, Texas" (Master's thesis, Texas Technological College, 1939), p. 69.

26. Dobie, *op. cit.,* p. 291.

27. Nunnalee to J.Q.A., reply to inquiry, 1960; Mattie D. Lucas, *A History of Grayson County, Texas* (Sherman, Texas, 1936), p. 68.

28. Leonie Weyand and Houston Wade, *An Early History of Fayette County* (La Grange, Texas, 1936).

29. Marwil to J.Q.A., reply to inquiry, 1960; Lelia A. Batte, *A History*

of Milam County (San Antonio, 1956); J. W. Gates and H. B. Fox, *A History of Leon County* (Centerville, Texas, 1936).

30. Gates and Fox, *op cit.*, p. 29.

31. Garland R. Farmer, *The Realm of Rusk County* (Henderson, Texas, 1951). Both derisive names, Lick Skillet and Nip and Tuck, were applied to Harmony Hill.

32. John R. Hutto, *Howard County in the Making* (privately printed, 1938).

33. A. W. Neville, *The History of Lamar County* (Paris, Texas, 1937), p. 42. Pinhook apparently was another fairly common facetious name. Lafayette, Louisiana, was first called Pin Hook, supposedly for a Frenchman who caught his neighbors' chickens with a grain of corn on a bent pin and served them in his restaurant. See William H. Perrin, *Southwest Louisiana* (New Orleans, 1891), pp. 183-84.

34. J. L. Stambaugh, *A History of Collin County* (Austin, 1958), p. 81.

35. Dobie, *op. cit.*, p. 292; H.B.T.

36. Thomas T. Ewell, *Hood County History* (Granbury, Texas, 1895; reprinted, 1956), p. 127.

37. Farmer, *op. cit.*; M. H. Marwil, Henderson, Texas, to J.Q.A.

38. H.B.T.; *Dallas Morning News*, November 24, 1960.

39. Charles D. Eaves and C. A. Hutchinson, *Post City, Texas: C. W. Post's Colonizing Activities in West Texas* (Austin, 1952).

40. Lora Blount, "A Short History of Fisher County" (Master's thesis, Hardin-Simmons University, 1947).

41. Brochure, Galveston Commercial Bank; Jessie L. Barfoot, "A History of McCulloch County" (Master's thesis, University of Texas, 1937), p. 129. The post office was changed to Pear Valley in 1910, not 1916 as Barfoot says.

42. William Harley Gandy, *A History of Montgomery County, Texas.*

43. Eulalie N. Wells, *Blazing the Way: Tales of Comanche County Pioneers* (Blanket, Texas, 1942), p. 33.

44. Clarence R. Wharton, *Wharton's History of Fort Bend County* (San Antonio, 1939), p. 224.

45. Hattie J. Roach, *A History of Cherokee County, Texas* (Dallas, 1934), p. 146.

46. Glyndon M. Riley, "The History of Hemphill County" (Master's thesis, West Texas State College, 1939), p. 14.

47. Roy Eddins, *History of Falls County, Texas.*

48. Pauline B. Hohes, *A Centennial History of Anderson County, Texas* (San Antonio, 1936), p. 248.

49. See, for example, "Tolbert's Texas," January 24 and January 31, 1960.

50. Mrs. Charles R. Morrison, Librarian, Collin County, reply to questionnaire, 1960.

51. Harrison to J.Q.A., reply to questionnaire, 1961.

52. H.B.T.; Dobie, *op. cit.*, p. 293.

53. Dobie, *op. cit.*, p. 288; H.B.T. erroneously lists 1881 as date of establishment of the post office.

54. Carrie J. Crouch, *A History of Young County* (Austin, 1956), p. 90.

55. Thomas T. Ewell, *Hood County History,* p. 52.

56. Frank X. Tolbert, "Tolbert's Texas," *Dallas Morning News,* March 13, 1960.

57. Reply to questionnaire, 1960.

58. Sid Cox, Department of English, Texas A. and M. College, native of Blanco County.

59. Max W. Fagg, "A Literary History of Collin County" (Master's thesis, East Texas State College, 1952), p. 50.

60. Velma Barrett, *Odessa: City of Dreams* (San Antonio, 1952), p. 114. Mrs. Vernice Hillier, Librarian, Ector County, says that the place was first known as TXL after oil was discovered on land belonging to the Texas Land and Cattle Company; it was also known as Caprock in 1946 but was changed to Notrees in April, 1947.

61. Baker, *op. cit.*, p. 167.

62. *Op. cit.*, p. 289.

63. Jonnie Ross Elzner, "The History of Lampasas County" (Master's thesis, Southwestern University, 1950), p. 237.

64. Jimmy Ann Hamm, paper written in Coldspring High School, 1949.

Cowboy Comedians and Horseback Humorists

PAUL PATTERSON

THE DAY of the old-time cowboy is long gone. You seldom see a cowboy a-horseback or a horse afoot these days—both commute to work in car and trailer.

The fact is, cowboying has become an indoor job strictly, a coliseum affair exclusively. Take for example the all-round cowboy champion of the world for 1960. A native of New York. He never came outdoors but twice all year long—once to take a sunbath and once to look at a cyclone cloud. His horse hasn't come out yet!

The same can be said of the cow, whose life is lived largely under a shed roof and who rides from calfhood to cannery. For example, the last herd I helped move any distance was some 850 yearling heifers we trailed from the Y Ranch to Odessa only thirty miles away. This took place in 1941. Now, just to show you how galloping deterioration has set in, if we—cowboys, horses, and cattle—were to attempt this trip today (only twenty years later) you'd have to treat the whole outfit, cowboys, horses, and cattle, for shock and exposure before we got a mile from headquarters!

To give you an idea, a couple of years back Crane City wanted me to take a covered wagon to Fort Stockton in commemoration of the Old Butterfield Stage Line's centennial. I flatly refused (having left Stockton in a covered wagon in 1921), but I agreed to try to locate a wagon and team, which later proved to be an impossible task. The chief problems were to locate two old-timers old enough to know how to hook up a team and still young and strong enough to lift the wagon tongue. Finally, we had to hire a couple of Hollywood hostlers and two horses broke to work. Eventually we found what we thought to be an ideal team, a span of perfectly matching grays (gray from age, we learned later, yet evidently not old enough to know the score). Every time we led them to the wagon tongue to hook on the breast yoke they would pull loose and break for the back of the wagon and jump in. A couple of commuters like the rest of us!

What with cowboys having quit the trails and gone to riding the channels, cowboy humor has fallen into the sere and the yellow leaf. Cowboy humor, like the cowboy himself, is a creation of Madison Avenue these days and as a result is as far-fetched and as phony as a foam-rubber saddle horn.

It is not only phony and flat, but delivered in an idiom as alien to the old-time cowboy as Richard Boone's characterizations are to any old-time cowboy I ever interviewed in my many years of close association with the Pecos River West. To give due credit, channel cowboys have deadlines to meet and therefore their humor can't be criticized too much for being cramped, but it shouldn't be foisted off on viewers as authentic.

But back to real old Western wit, horseback humor, cowboy comedy—stories I have never yet seen in print, but the kind I heard, both first and second hand, the first fifteen or twenty years of my life. As a boy growing up around Upland (a town now dead and gone from Upton County) I was privileged to sit at the feet of one of the greatest wits of that time, Lee Reynolds, Cow Boy (then spelled with two capital letters, which even then didn't do justice to Lee either as cowboy or as humorist).

Some say that wit, like good, aged whiskey, is a long long time in the making; it comes hard but goes down easy. All I know is that Lee Reynolds is still quoted where old-time cowboys gather. Too, I do know that Lee Reynolds, like a good many of his contemporaries, has been known to coyote it in some lonesome line camp for as high as six or eight months at a stretch without laying eye on man, woman, or child. This could be the secret of Lee's success as a sage. He had plenty of time to ponder points and temper timing.

Living in that long and lonesome land, after so many years cowboys became somewhat woman-shy—a fear which they invariably tried to disguise as contempt. (Actually, a startling majority of them died bachelors.) Such was the case with Lee. Anyhow, one night Lee was camped at Powell Gap and had as a guest a surveyor who was laying out the right-of-way for the now defunct Orient Railroad (K.C. M. & O.). Now, the paucity of people made for a plenitude of panthers (or vice versa), and along about bedtime something opened up a blood-clabbering scream.

"My God," said the surveyor, coming straight up out of his soogans, "I hope that isn't a panther!"

Lee's voice, just as terrified, came back through the darkness: "Igod, I hope it ain't a woman!"

To compensate for his fear of women, good or bad (most especially good), he catered somewhat and sometimes to whiskey good or bad. And hereon hangs the next tale.

The JM outfit had a big herd "throwed in" on water at Boykin Tank up on King Mountain, and, it being around three of a summer evening, Lee was what he would call "mighty dry for water." His was an overwhelming thirst incurred partially by eleven hours in the saddle, but mostly by the satisfaction of an earlier thirst in Rankin the night before. Easing his way around and through the herd, he rode his horse belly deep into the slimy, soupy, cow-flavored, horse-savored water and slurped down several hatfulls. Then he turned to Charley Lyons, who had just ridden up.

"Charley," he said, clearing his throat as he was wont to do, what with words coming so seldom, "I wisht I had me a jug. I'd send my old mother a jug of this water!" Charley, of course, nodded gravely, having been with Lee all day—and the night before.

At Galveston, when Lee got his first glimpse of the Gulf of Mexico he cleared his throat and allowed as how it "would be a hell of a good place to water a herd."

Up in Odessa one time, what with Lee feeling his corn (distilled, cowboy equivalent of his oats), he had Old Rowdy girted up tight, a sizable loop built, and was waiting for the T & P passenger train to pull in—or out. Either way he was going to rope the smokestack.

"Lee," pleaded one of the "Clabber Hill" hands, "don't do it. You don't know what you're a-ropin'!"

"Ahhhh. No, and they don't know what I'm a-ridin' either."

Most of Lee Reynolds' escapades had something to do with cattle or horses or whiskey or all three. Once down in Rankin he was a guest at the only hotel in town—a place run by a thrifty German woman who put a light accent on the English language but a very heavy accent on seriousness and solemnity and hard work at all times. Foolishness was for fools, mirth for morons. One morning her milk cow, which she kept staked to the windmill tower, showed up missing. Right off she knew whom to suspect.

"Lhee Reynoldts, where's my milk cow at?"

"Ahhhm," says Lee, pulling his ever-present tally book from a vest pocket. "What's her yere-mark? Her brand? I'll get 'er in the spring roundup."

Grabbing up a double handful of Lee Reynolds, the big, powerful landlady stepped to the back door and threw Lee as far as she could send him (which as Lee himself put it was "a right smart ways").

Raising up on one elbow, the ejected, dejected cowboy

surveyed the lay of the land and the landlady somewhat sadly.

"Ahhhhm. That's a hell of a way to run a hotel!"

Next we hear of Lee up in some little town in New Mexico at what we now call a rodeo. He is leaning on the counter of a concession stand which is being manned by women —a Ladies' Auxiliary of some sort. Obviously he had enough of wine to deaden that gnawing fear of women.

"And what can we do for you, sir?" asked one of the ladies politely.

"Awww, gimme a water-dog san'witch. Right frash outta the float valve."

Lee Reynolds' peer as a wit—he had no peer as a cowboy, it was said—was probably Bud Colbaugh, who headquartered at San Angelo. Bud, in this day and time, would doubtless prove the greatest stand-up comedian around (the only drawback being, when old Bud was at his best he was in no condition to stand up).

He, like Lee on occasions, liked long looks at the sky with a quart bottle as a telescope. During early prohibition, when whiskey could be obtained only through a doctor's prescription, Bud had the extreme good fortune to get bit by a rattlesnake. However, time and strict adherence to the doctor's prescription cured Bud completely of snakebite. Even so, he kept going back for more medicine, but the doctor kept turning him down. Early one morning a neighbor noticed Bud out at the woodpile juggling mesquite around to beat the band.

"Bud, I know you better'n that. You ain't about to cut no wood."

"Oh, hell no!"

"Then what're ye up to?"

"I'm looking fer me another snake."

It so happened that in better days Bud's best friend in San Angelo was a bartender, in Bud's point of view the only type of friend worth cultivating. And it so happened that one day this bartender friend called upon Bud to eject a mean Irishman from his place of business.

"Why don't you thow him out?" asked Bud.

"He's an old schoolmate of mine."

Believing he could "thow" him out, most especially after one or two of the bartender's best under his belt, Bud went in after him.

Shortly there was considerable commotion inside, and here came Bud on all fours—and much of his considerable momentum wasn't of his own making.

"Dammit, Bud, whyn't ye throw him out?"

"Aw, I found out he was an old schoolmate of mine too!"

As Bud's reputation grew, his repertoire of stories likewise increased.

Booger Red Privitt, the famous bronc rider, one of Bud's contemporaries, was jealous of the title "ugliest man in the world." In fact, Booger Red had boasted that he'd shoot the first fellow he ever saw uglier'n he was, which boast he made to Bud Colbaugh the first time they met.

Bud studied Booger a minute, shifted his cud to the other jaw and said, "Feller, if I'm uglier than you air you don't have to shoot me. I'll do it myself."

When asked where he was born Bud reported that he "come out of a live oak thicket down in Kimble County."

Bud died in San Angelo some ten years back, unwept, unhonored, and unsung, yet it would take a book—and an interesting one—to set down all the saws and the sayings of the likes of him.

Old Man Harry Wade was a longtime hand of the 7D's and later the OH Triangles, a seven-hundred-section spread owned by the Sugg Estate in Irion County. Old Man Harry was noted for a pungent, piercing, hide-peeling irony—a sort of cynical sarcasm aimed at the faults and failings and foibles of both horse and human. (He too lived and died a bachelor.)

But unlike Bud or Lee, Old Harry didn't seek out an audience. Most of his was soliloquy, meant only for himself or his horse. One day he had tried for a considerable time to hem a horse up and bridle him (he didn't believe in roping out his mounts as the young hands did). About the time he'd get the old pony's ears in the headstall the critter would wheel and run off. Finally old Harry threw his bridle at the skittish critter and stalked off muttering to himself, "God made man king of all beasts. And made ever' dam one of 'em to outrun him!"

Another time, to show his contempt for a teenie-weenie team of Mexican mules Old Man Sugg had bought, he threw them out one small handful of oats and said, "There, dam ye, now bust yoreselves."

And then there was Mose Rucker who worked for the 6's out of Sherwood back in the nineties. Mose Rucker, typical of the cowboy of the time, hoot-owled it seven or eight months at a time without ever setting foot inside a settlement. And when he did come in he was cursed with a long thirst, which he quenched first. Mose had just stepped out of a saloon and there stood the town cobbler—a hunchback, leaning away forward. Mose, standing a bit straighter, but by no means steadier, studied the leaning man for quite some time. Finally his expression of puzzlement turned to exasperation.

"Dammit," he rasped out, "if'n you're a-gonna jump, *jump!*"

Although not of the stature of Bud Colbaugh or Lee Reynolds as horseback humorists, many other old-timers have been good for at least one story that has stood the test of time and telling. One such story is said to have originated in Sheffield fifty, sixty, or seventy years ago in Sam Murry's saloon. It seems that a drummer was in there enjoying a quiet drink when a cowboy, wheeling his horse away from the bar, caused the critter to stomp on the drummer's foot. Immediately the drummer took his complaint to the bartender, who was Sam Murry himself. But there was no sympathy, much less compensation, forthcoming from Sam.

"What the hell you a-doin' in here afoot anyhow?" he asked.

A couple of other such stories come out of Fort Stockton, likewise by word of mouth. The first one had to do with the cowboy who used to come in from some big outfit out of town a good ways, tie his horse in front of the first saloon, and proceed to have a look at the elephant and listen to the lobo.

One day the boys sneaked out and turned his saddle around. Directly out wobbles the cowboy and climbs into the saddle. But something seems amiss? Nope. Here's the saddle horn. And the stirrups? But hold up, here. Where's Old Rambler's head at? Looking quite confused, not to say abused, the cowboy steps back down, reties his horse, steps back and kicks the critter a resounding boot in the belly. "Now, you old so and so! Ain't you ashamed of yoreself? Now stan' there till you sober up!"

Finally, the one that has to do with the late Snaky Price. Snaky was on drive one morning when he jumped a big black bear. He built hisself a loop, loped to the bear, and fit it on him right quick. Then he turned and rode the other way. When he looked back he noticed that the bear was coming up the rope, hand over hand. Then, spiter'n hell and all he could do, the bear clumb up and kicked him out of the saddle. Smoky hit the ground a-runnin' and when he looked back this bear was shakin' his ownself out a loop. Snaky says if he hadn't beat the dam thang to a rough header he reckon the bear'd a roped him and drug him slap to death!

Back when man had to make his own amusements—when absolutely nothing was imported but sowbelly, beans, and Arbuckle coffee—pranks, tricks, and even tales were time-tested, tempered, and tampered with until they were masterpieces of delight, at least for the authors thereof. And there was time for the telling and retelling, and there was solitude enough for contemplation, and there were rehearsals enough for mastery of the lines.

Long gone are Lee Reynolds, Bud Colbaugh, Mose Rucker, Old Man Harry Wade, and that bunch, but by whatever lost campfire they squat today you can bet somebody hunkered thereabout is laughing, even unto the cook, given up to be the crabbiest, crankiest critter this side of a grizzly bear. And it won't be canned laughter, imported humor, but the real McCoy both ways.

Superstitions in Vermilion Parish

ELIZABETH BRANDON

THERE ARE two obvious ways for a folklorist to collect superstitions: to live in a given region and observe the daily life
and mores of the inhabitants, and to ask pertinent questions,
hoping they will be answered. These two methods may not
be sufficient, however, since country folk, who are often suspicious of intruders, are likely to change or hide some customs
when they think they are being watched and to withdraw
into silence when questions are asked of them. Then there
is a third way, less obvious but still significant, and that is
to collect legends. Any good storyteller will gladly keep on
spinning yarns on subjects familiar to him, and sooner or later
he will tell tales of witchcraft, ghosts, spectral ships, buried
treasures, haunted houses, and metamorphoses. These stories
will usually be told in the third person, about things that
happened to someone else or that someone else believed in
long ago. A further check and a more careful study of the facts
at the folklorist's disposal will then reveal that a number of
these beliefs are still current. I have used all three methods
in collecting superstitious beliefs in Vermilion Parish, one of
the French parishes of southwestern Louisiana.[1]

The first thing the observer asks about the old beliefs
still very much alive in this part of Louisiana is why they
have survived so vigorously in this age of electronics and
atomic energy. The answer lies in the milieu and in the
mentality of the inhabitants. The utter isolation of the bayou

country before 1920, the scarcity of schools, and the lack of roads and means of transportation in the area were instrumental in the preservation of the Cajuns' old way of life and, with it, of many old beliefs.

The superstitions still encountered among the Cajuns stem mainly from two origins, French and Negro, which intermingled on the Louisiana soil. The Acadians who landed upon the black islands in the Caribbean, says Hewitt L. Ballowe, "were saturated with belief in jungle magic, the effiicacy of charms." In Louisiana, "they drifted naturally into the marsh. . . . They reverted to teachings of the church, but naïvely clung to the charms and fetishes of the cult."[2] Harnett Kane, who has also studied this aspect of Cajun traditions, says of the two sources: "The Negroes have brought their superstitions, largely from Africa and to them the whites, for the most part the French, have joined their own. A lush mixture has resulted with members of both races and all shadings enjoying a rich spirit world about them."[3]

That the isolated stretches of marshland where the Acadians settled were propitious to the survival of the old and to the development of new superstitions is not surprising. "If you have ever been alone on a bayou with woods on both sides of you," writes Hilda Roberts, "and heard the weird screech of an owl, even in the day time, you can easily understand how a simple Cajun or negro, hearing the sound at night, would feel that danger threatened and try to avert it."

It is interesting to note the paucity of legends pertaining to apparitions of saints, of the Virgin Mary and Jesus, of angels and good fairies. In the collections of folksongs and folktales, too, the religious motif is—with a few exceptions—conspicuously lacking. The belief in impish *lutins* and harmless mermaids is nonexistent, while horror tales of conjuration, gris-gris, and ghosts abound.

It is generally thought that the belief in conjuration is exclusively of Negro-African origin. And yet, when we read

of important studies of European scholars on witchcraft or
when we follow the findings of European folklorists, or for
that matter of American folklorists who have done their
research among white people where there is no Negro influence,
we come to the conclusion that witchcraft is of European as
well as of Negro-African origin, although certain external
aspects of conjuration attest to pure African retention.

There is a popular opinion that conjuration is practiced
mostly among Negroes. This is not the case in Vermilion, for
I found there many white people who believe in conjurers,
and who use conjuration charms and fear their power. The
collections of folklorists like Vance Randolph and Richard
Dorson who carried on their research in other parts of the
country among whites not in contact with Negroes bear out
my observations.

Another idea commonly held is that there is a negative
correlation between education and belief in witchcraft. We
have a tendency to think that a person with a certain amount
of education will not believe in superstitions. But again, this
is not the case in Vermilion. In 1940 William Seabrook said,
"All primitives and more than half the literate white popu-
lation in the world today believe in witchcraft."[5] While this
proportion does not hold in Vermilion, we must nevertheless
admit that there are literate whites in the parish who are
addicted to witchcraft.[6]

In Vermilion everyone knows stories about conjurers who
claim to possess supernatural powers, and about their gris-
gris or "conjos."[7] When a person is said to be conjured, it
means that a spell is cast on him and something is bound
to happen to him. The powers of conjuration charms are
varied: they attract or force lovers to return to each other,
they protect from diseases, they assure a woman's beauty;
they bring pleasant dreams or good luck in gambling; and
they can also bring bad luck to harm, torment, or even kill
an enemy. Protective and good luck charms[8] are worn on the

neck or wrist, carried in pockets, or sewn on clothing. The
malevolent charms are hidden somewhere in the victim's
house—in closets, pillows, drawers, and dark corners, and
under mattresses and beds. Outside, they are hidden in flower
beds and shrubbery.

These fetishes can be made from alligator teeth, grains
of plants, a cord with three, seven, or nine knots in it, or a
little bag, preferably made of red flannel and filled with
such so-called magic substances as nail-clippings, feathers,
human or animal hair, or such weird ingredients as dried
nerves from the wings of a vulture, snake bones, powdered
dried snakeskin, dirt or dust collected at the cemetery, or
rust from nails or rusty tacks or pins. Strong-smelling items—
mustard grains, asafetida, or garlic—are sometimes added.

Other, less complicated gris-gris consist of charmed candy
or other food items put in front of the victim. Stories are told
of people who, as a result of eating the food gris-gris, became
tracassés (crazy) or *possédés* (possessed), or simply withered
away and died.

These charms are usually purchased from a conjurer, who
is called in the parish a "hoodoo man." Some gris-gris can
be produced, however, without the aid of a hoodoo man; one
need only know the magic formula. Here is one that any
woman can prepare. In order to attract a man's attention in
the café or at a dance, a woman should prick her finger
with a pin. When a drop of blood comes out of the finger,
she should put it on a stick of gum and give it to the man
of her choice. If he chews it, he will not be able to resist her.

Some charms can be purchased in drugstores:

If you know where to go, there are drugstores in many of the larger
towns where you can buy Love Powders, Get-Together Drops, Boss Fix
Powder, Come-to-me Powder, Devil Oil, Controlling Oil and Dice
Special. If you are white and prosperous, your cook may have better
luck in obtaining the charm you desire.[9]

When one is threatened with conjuration or believes that

a gris-gris has been hidden in his house, he can always get a counteragent from a hoodoo doctor. A good way to stop a gris-gris from acting is either to walk around the house with a lighted blessed candle or to throw salt in the corners of each room where the suspect has been. Many cases of conjuration are told about in the parish and elsewhere. Here are three that were told me by various informants:

"It was in my brother-in-law's family. He had a daughter who lost her mind. In one of her mattresses they found a powder which fell on the linens and the powder was so strong that it tore the linens. The girl lost her mind after that. They never knew who put it there but they believed that it was a boy who wanted her to love him."[10]

"A man I know told me that his wife was very sick because a neighbor of hers gave her a gris-gris. When I asked him how they knew that the gris-gris had caused her sickness, he answered that they found little packages with pins and hair under her mattress, in the drawers and in the yard. They called a doctor, who did not do her any good. The only thing to do was to give her another gris-gris that would counteract the first gris-gris. So they went to a hoodoo man who was making such gris-gris. They got one, brought it to this man's wife, and she got well. They really believe in those things, those people."[11]

"A classmate of mine from a home economics class at the University of Houston, a woman in her late thirties, told me about how unhappy she was that her seventeen-year-old daughter had fallen in love with a young man that she, the mother, objected to. She mentioned the fact that she might go to Louisiana to get a powder that she had heard about which was supposed to make the young man shy away from the girl. This was before the end of the school year. In the fall, when I saw her again, I asked her at what stage was her daughter's romance. She beamed and told me that she had gone to Louisiana, had bought the powder for about $10.00, had put it in a little bag and had sewn it under the collar of the girl's jacket. According to her, the powder worked very fast and within a week or so the young man and her daughter got into a fight and stopped going out together. About a year later, when I saw her again, she told me that she was seriously thinking of going back to Louisiana and buying a new kind of powder, this one to attract a man she herself would like to marry since she has been a divorcée for some time."[12]

Three other episodes are particularly significant because they show the part played by gris-gris in the daily life of the community today. The first, dealing with sympathetic magic, was related to me by a friend who is a high-school teacher in Vermilion Parish. A girl student of hers showed her an effigy she had received in a package from a former boy friend who had refused to accept the fact that she had become interested in someone else. It was a doll with hair and eyes the color of the girl's. A hatpin was stuck where the heart should be.

The second episode took place in the house of a family of friends, where a conjure bag was found in a closet. Upon investigation it was revealed that the bag had been placed there by the girl friend of one of the young sons of the household. The girl took this means of bringing back her boy friend, who had stopped calling on her.[13]

Third, some acquaintances of mine who own rental property quite often resort to gris-gris when they want to get rid of an undesirable tenant. They make seven knots in a cord, tie some hair on it, sprinkle some black pepper or paprika over it, and hang it on the entrance door of the apartment. The tenant disappears overnight. I was assured that this device never failed.

Ghosts, called *morts* or *revenants*, still inhabit the parish. As in European traditions, they are believed to be the tormented souls of the dead, who for one reason or another were condemned to come back to earth. One belief of "English extraction," quoted by Newbill Niles Puckett[14] and known in the parish, is that only people born with a cowl can see ghosts. An informant told me a story containing this belief:

"My mother could see ghosts. They used to come wake her up when she was asleep. When she used to go to spend an evening at the neighbor's, on the way back she'd see a man who was following them who wanted to get into the buggy or catch the horse by the bridle. So she'd tell Pop: 'Stop, stop, there is a man following us.' He'd stop but he wouldn't see anything. It was a ghost that was coming back to earth that she could see because she was born with a cowl."[15]

Many parallels can be established between the ghost beliefs of Vermilion Parish and those of other parts of the United States or of Europe. I found a variation, however, in the testimonies of a few of the older people, who assured me that when they were children they used to be threatened with tales of *revenants* who would come and carry them off if they did not behave. Another generally unknown aspect of the *revenant* appears in the following testimony, given to me in full faith and seriousness by my informant, a thirty-five-year-old Negro maid.

"The ghosts of the dead often come back to this world to torture people. If you kill someone not rightfully, then the ghost of the dead man comes back to bother you, you start seeing blood on your hands and in your food. You cannot eat, you cannot sleep, all you do is think about the man you killed and finally it gets you, you become like crazy, you lose your mind. But if you kill someone rightfully, the ghost won't bother you.

"One of my uncles, the one who married my mother's youngest sister, had a disagreement with another man while they played cards. So he went after his gun, he came back and then he got on a chair (he was so little that he had to get on a chair), he fired and he killed the other man. Everybody thought that the ghost would come after him and that my uncle would destroy himself, but we should believe that he killed him rightfully because until now the ghost never came."[16]

When I asked what happened to her uncle, my informant looked at me with naïve seriousness and answered, "Nothing happened to him. As I told you, the ghost did not come, he did not see blood in his food, he has been eating and sleeping well for years, and today he is real fat."

Somewhat less important is the belief in the will-o'-the-wisp, the *feu-follet*. In general type the *feu-follet* of Vermilion Parish resembles that of the French. The *fifollet*, as they call it in Louisiana, is the soul of a dead person which has been sent by God back to earth to do penance, but which instead plays nasty tricks on people, annoying them and scaring them at night. It can also be a soul haunting its grave in the cemetery because it cannot get to paradise or because it has escaped from purgatory. A common Louisiana belief, very prevalent in Vermilion, is that a *fifollet* is the soul of a child who died before he was baptized. In the form of a will-o'-the-wisp he keeps haunting the place where he lived all too short a time, hoping that people will pray for him so that he may find his way to heaven. Like Puckett's Jack-o'-my-lantern,[17] the *fifollet* leads people into bogs, swamps, or the bayou. Like the French Canadian *feu follet*,[18] it can go through the eye of a needle; and as in Canada a good way to get rid of it is to stick it with a knife against a tree trunk or a pole. Occasionally, the Louisiana *fifollet* may be a vampire who is out to suck people's blood. Worst of all, its desire may be for the blood of a child.[19]

The age-old belief in metamorphosis, as prevalent as the belief in witches among whites and Negroes alike, surviving as the idea of the *loup-garou* in Europe and among the French in

Canada and in other parts of Louisiana,[20] is quite unknown in Vermilion. No one had any story to tell me about a witch who assumed the shape of a cat, wolf, crow, or some other animal or bird, to do evil to her enemies, and then in her human form the next day displayed the ill effects of having been injured while in the form of the animal. The *loup-garou*, pronounced *roup-garou*, is indeed well known in the parish, but it has an entirely different meaning. All my informants repeated the same thing—that a *roup-garou* is a malefactor, a man who does bad, sneaky, underhanded things, a man to be avoided:

"A *roup-garou* is an individual who does annoying and underhanded things, you know. In the evening he goes here and there, he watches and looks everywhere. And at dawn, early in the morning, he is already up, waiting. Nobody knows that it is he. A *roup-garou* is a malefactor, a sort of trouble-maker . . . a suspicious individual in the evening. It is usually an ordinary man, but he is sneaky in his ways, he is every-where, looking for things, annoying."[21]

To children the *roup-garou* is a boogeyman who, like a *revenant,* will come and get them if they are bad. Mrs. Henry Saltzman of Gueydan told me, "When we were little, if some-thing bad happened, mother used to say: 'It must be a *roup-garou* who is the cause of it.' Maybe it was to make us afraid."[22]

It is evident to the collector that some superstitions like those pertaining to the *loup-garou* and the *feu-follet* tend to disappear gradually with the passing of older residents and the advance of education. There is also a noticeable paucity, in the Vermilion of today, of beliefs in good fairies and miracles performed by saints, so prominent in European and French Canadian folklore. And yet the superstitions based on fear and black magic persist. The reason for this lies in the influence which stems from Africa. The African Negro, having had in his homeland a religion based primarily on fear, remained pro-foundly attached to the vestiges of the supernatural conceptions of magic and fetishism which he continued to practice in the New World. The Cajun brought his own belief in witchcraft, but this would no doubt have survived only in a very mild form had it not been for the Negro influence which so greatly emphasized it. The impact of this vigorous and convincing Negro superstition left an indelible imprint on all who came in contact with it, and it overshadowed all other beliefs. As a result, horror superstitions far outweighed the less frightening beliefs, as well as the expressions of faith and trust in religious figures and symbols.

To what extent do people of our era believe in these superstitions? We are tempted to answer, "more than we would think"; for if high-school and college students still practice conjuration, if it is still possible to buy magic powders in drugstores, if a man who has committed a murder believes he is absolved of the crime because the ghost of the dead man has not come to torture him, we are forced to conclude that superstitions still have great power in our world today.

1. This article is based on materials collected mostly among Cajuns in Vermilion Parish in the years 1950-55.

2. Hewett L. Ballowe, *Creole Folk Tales* (Baton Rouge, 1948), p. x.

3. Harnett T. Kane, *Deep Delta Country* (New York, 1944), p. 245.

4. Hilda Roberts, "Louisiana Superstitions," *Journal of American Folklore*, XL (1927), 146.

5. William Seabrook, *Witchcraft, Its Power in the World Today* (New York, 1940), p. 7.

6. In his *Ozark Superstitions* (New York, 1947), Vance Randolph claims that one of the biggest witch doctors he knew was a prominent physician.

7. "*Conjuration, conjurer, conjah.* Terms used by Negroes of the United States for the process of working magic, the worker of magic and magic itself." *Funk and Wagnalls Standard Dictionary of Folklore, Mythology and Legend* (New York, 1949), p. 247.

"*Grigri.* The term for magic charms used by French writers and applied especially to West Africa. All the reservations entered on the use of the word *fetish* apply in equal measure to employing this term in meaningful description." *Ibid.*, p. 466.

"The word 'gri-gri' as it has come down to us in Louisiana has lost something of its original African sense and has come to have almost the same significance as hoodoo ... meaning to put an evil spell on a person or enterprise through charms, incantations, etc." The African meaning of *gri-gri* is talisman, charm, or fetish. Laura L. Porteous, "The Gri-Gri Case," *Louisiana Historical Quarterly,* XVII (1934), 50. *Conjo* and *gris-gris* seem to be synonymous in Louisiana.

8. A coin may be a good luck charm. A priest in the parish told me that parishioners often come to ask him to bless a coin which they would like to use as a fetish. He refuses these requests.

9. *Louisiana: A Guide to the State* (New York, 1945), p. 99.

10. Mrs. Henry Saltzman, Gueydan, Louisiana.

11. Mrs. Courtney LeBauve, Abbeville, Louisiana. I should like to take this opportunity to thank my devoted friends, the Henry Saltzman family and Mrs. LaBauve, for the valuable help they gave me while I was working in Vermilion Parish.

12. Mrs. Paule Carroll, Houston, Texas, 1961. This testimony was given to Mrs. Carroll within the last two years. Stories of this kind are legion in this part of the country. A few years ago, newspapers reported the indictment and trial in Houston of a Mrs. Bishop, who was selling miraculous powders in her drugstores. Another interesting story which appeared in the newspapers was that of a conjure bag found by a southern college football team in their players' dormitory.

13. Vance Randolph, *Ozark Superstitions* (New York, 1947), p. 8. Randolph quotes a parallel case: "And there was a pretty girl once, a senior at one of our best Ozark colleges, who obtained her heart's desire by a semi-public 'conjuration' which would not seem out of place in a medieval book on demonology."

14. Newbill Niles Puckett, *Folk Beliefs of the Southern Negro* (Chapel Hill, 1926), p. 137.

15. Mrs. Celestine Morton, Negro, Kaplan, Louisiana.

16. For obvious reasons I cannot reveal the name of my informant.

17. Puckett, *op. cit.,* p. 134.

18. Marius Barbeau, "Anecdotes populaires du Canada," *Journal of American Folklore,* XXXIII (1920), 201-2.

19. In two unpublished Louisiana Creole tales, "Fin Fifole" and "Fifole," in Remi Lavergne, "A Phonetic Transcription of the Creole Negro's Medical Treatments, Superstitions, and Folklore in the Parish of Pointe Coupée" (Master's thesis, Louisiana State University, 1930), the two *feux-follets* are vampires who suck the blood of children.

20. Kane, *op. cit.,* pp. 220-22.

21. Henry Saltzman, Gueydan, Louisiana.

22. Mrs. Henry Saltzman, Gueydan, Louisiana.

The Changing Concept of the Negro Hero

ROGER ABRAHAMS

EACH PIECE of collected lore from any group must be considered as a synchronism, triggering simultaneous responses on many levels within both the performer and his audience, touching both the existence of the individuals involved and their relationship to society. This is especially true when dealing with narrative lore. The performers (and the individuals in the audience through their involvement and approbation) achieve a certain kind of anxiety release by the externalization of some of their otherwise unutterable or unexpressed significant thoughts and actions. Closely related to this, the narrative may function in order to give sanction to the values of the group, and thus to provide a guide for future actions. Further, certain anxieties may exist on both an individual and a group level, due to a specific situation of a group within a larger society. In other words, by laughing at, railing at, perhaps even just mentioning some of the excesses or inequities of life, a piece of folklore can salve some of the wounds created by these problems.

The anxieties which exist for the lower-class Negro male, which are created by social impediments and which cause serious detours in the process of individuation, are mirrored in the levels on which they are expressed in his lore. His situation as a poor man, as a male in a society in which his women can find work and status more easily than he, and as a black man in a white man's society causes physical,

119

historical, social, and psychological repercussions. Narratives collected from a group of young Negroes in South Philadelphia indicate the terms in which the anxieties resulting from these situations are expressed, and perhaps alleviated to a certain degree. Certain elements are common to a number of the narratives.

As all these social problems unite to dislocate the egos of the young men, it should come as no surprise that the most dominant aspect of the point of view of the narrative pieces is the insistent note of the personal involvement of the narrator in the story. Just as one can see the function of much lore of the urban Negro as the attempt of one individual to best another, so in the stories we can discern a similar accent upon the role of the performer in the importance of the narrative *persona* expressed in a device called, for want of a better term, the "intrusive 'I.'"

Throughout the narratives we are conscious of a close relationship between the hero of the tale and the person doing the narration. In most cases, especially in the toasts, the point of view is strictly first person, allowing the complete identification of narrator and hero. In others, this identification is put at a slight remove by placing the narration in the third person, but allowing the hero some attribute by which one can identify him with the narrator (a colored man competing with members of other races, a man of words in a dupable group, etc.).

This "intrusive 'I'" is a convenient gambit in the narrative game. It allows the narrator two *personae* at the same time, his own as narrator or commentator and that of the hero. He can unite the two at will if he is artful in his narration; he can also dissociate the two if he wishes. It is important in certain stories that he be able to vary his position, as there will be actions which he (the narrator) will not approve, or situations in which he would not want to be found. As opposed to the classic English and Scottish ballads, there is nothing removed, long ago, impersonal about these narratives. Even when the narrator's *persona* retreats from that of the hero or main character, the narrator remains, intruding as a commentator. The "I" never disappears completely, though it may occasionally recede temporarily.[1]

With what sort of heroes do these men identify themselves? This question is especially important as the action patterns of the heroes will dictate the values which the narrator is espousing. In the broad view of the narratives, the heroes fit into two major categories, the trickster (or "clever hero") and the badman (or a special type of "contest hero").

The trickster figure has been the most identified hero in Negro lore throughout this country and the West Indies. This is perhaps due to a real prevalence of this type character in Negro story. On the other hand, it may be because Joel Chandler Harris noticed the similarities between European animal trickster tales and those found among the southern Negroes, and collected and printed many of these stories in his Uncle Remus books. His success with these works may have influenced future collections of the same type.[2]

At any rate, we can no longer claim that the trickster figure is the only, or even the dominating, hero type encountered in Negro tales. But he is still to be encountered among the Negroes in the guise of the "Signifying Monkey," the "colored man," "John," and (sometimes) the preacher.[3]

The trickster or "clever hero" is one who triumphs or functions by means of his wits. Or as Orrin Clapp has noted in the *Journal of American Folklore:*

> He either vanquishes or escapes from a formidable opponent by a ruse. The clever hero is usually smaller and weaker than those with whom he is matched, frequently being a diminutive animal. The victory of the clever hero is the perennial triumph of brains over brawn, *la sagesse des petits.*[4]

Perhaps the *petit* quality to which Clapp refers has implications beyond matters of size. The trickster figure functions in society not at all like a small animal; he functions like a small human being, a child. His delight in tricking is reminiscent of the similar pleasure children derive from tricking their peers. Indeed, in almost every sense the trickster is a child. He has no perceptible set of values except the demands of his ego (in the disguise of his id). One could not say that he is immoral; he is, rather, amoral, because he exists in the stage before morality has had a chance to inculcate itself upon his being. He is "the spirit of disorder, the enemy of boundaries."[5] "Although he is not really evil," says C. G. Jung (i.e., against established order or morality), "he does the most atrocious things from sheer unconsciousness and unrelatedness."[6] He is an individual just beginning on the quest for identity; "A minatory and ridiculous figure, he stands at the very beginning of the way of individuation."[7]

The existence of this amoral, this childlike, hero[8] creates important questions. If the narrative functions both as an expression of otherwise repressed anxieties[9] and as a "tutor, the shaper of identities," why has the Negro chosen to represent himself and his values as childlike? There are a number of possible answers. In the guise of the small (childlike) animal, the Negro is perhaps fulfilling the role in which he has been cast by his white "masters" (the childish "Uncle Tom" who is convinced of his simple state and thus needs the protection of his masters). At the same time, in this role he is able to show a superiority over those larger or more important than himself through his tricks, thus partially salving his wounded ego. This is apparent in the "Marster-John" cycles where he is tricking the white man, or in the Br'er Rabbit stories where he is getting the better of larger animals. This might be the function of the trickster on the sociological level: a veiled reaction against overdomination while preserving the role in which he has been cast.

The psychological satisfaction of the trickster story is similar. As Melville Herskovits says of the trickster figure in general:

"Psychologically the role of the trickster seems to be that of projecting the insufficiencies of man in his universe onto a smaller creature, who in besting his larger adversaries, permits the satisfaction of an obvious identification to those who recount or listen to these stories."[10] The trickster, then, may represent to the Negro, through identification, the small, often assailed hero in control of his world through guile (the only defense available to the Negro under the slave and the post-slave system).

But it is not the trickster's smallness or his guile which really provides the Negro with his greatest source of anxiety release. It is his amorality. Reaction against authority, the white man's word and law, is forbidden. But this revolt is very important to the psychic growth of the individual. The only rebellion available then is through the actions of a figure who has undergone an (apparent) regression to the childlike state where he is not responsible for his actions because he has not yet learned the difference between right and wrong. His acts are unconscious, therefore extend beneath (or above) his ability to make choices. "He is both subhuman and superhuman, a bestial and divine being, whose chief and most alarming characteristic is his unconsciousness."[11] His then is the rampant ego, the ego without the confines of the prison of society, because it exists in the permissive world accorded to other childish individuals. The trickster provides a full escape for those Negroes who have been offered no opportunity to feel a control over their own lives, no method for developing their egos through specific action. As such, the trickster may reflect the real childlike state of a severely stunted ego, or a veiled revolt against authority in the only terms available. At the same time the performer and audience are enabled to express some of their destructive impulses in this acceptable form.

But the badman, not the trickster, is the most popular hero among these Negroes. The badman represents a conception quite different from the trickster. He is, in many ways, a "contest hero": ". . . the [contest] hero is placed in the position of publicly defeating all rivals. The winner is acclaimed hero or champion. The rivalry may be in skill, fortitude, virtue, or in main strength but such proof of the hero by contest with other humans is almost universal."[12]

The badmen of this group, "Stackolee," "The Great Mac-Daddy," Jesse and Frank James, are like the classic conception of the "contest hero" in that they are powerful, do overcome all rivals, and are (secretly) acclaimed as heroes because of their strength and will. This is almost the point where the resemblance ceases, for the badman does not seem to work for the benefit of society.

Where the trickster is a perpetual child, the badman is a perpetual adolescent. His is a world of overt rebellion. He commits acts against taboos and mores in full knowledge of what he is doing. In fact, he glories in this knowledge of revolt. He is consciously and sincerely immoral. As a social entity he is rebelling against white man's laws. As a male he is revolting against woman's attempt to emasculate him. As a poor man he is reacting against his perpetual poverty.

But his ego is not unbridled like the trickster's; rather, it is directed, though not in positive terms as in the usual contest hero, but rather against anything which attempts to constrain him. His expression of his ego is his physical prowess. He is the strong man, who, because of his strength, accepts the challenges of the world. He is ruler through his powers and anything which threatens his domain threatens his ego and must be removed. Where guile and banter are the weapons of the trickster, arrogance and disdain serve the badman. He does not aim to be a god, but rather to be the eternal man in revolt, the devil.

The rebellion against authority exemplified in the badman is much more overt than that in the trickster. Here we have the open defiance which we are able to see exhibited in real life among the Negroes in the activities of their gangs and the establishment of their gang leaders, and, with some of them, later in their lives as criminals. The values of this group in revolt are implied in the conduct of their badman heroes. Life, as well as lore, admits a more open expression of revolt than in the past, and this is echoed in the nature of the heroes worshiped by these Negroes.

Perhaps it would be more instructive to apply some of these generalizations to specific narratives. Let us first look at a tale of a trickster, "The Signifying Monkey and the Lion."

The opening makes it clear what sort of creature the monkey is:

> Deep down in the jungle, so they say
> There's a signifying monkey down the way.
> There hadn't been no disturbing in the jungle for quite a bit,
> For up jumped the monkey in the tree one day and laughed,
>   "I guess I'll start some stuff."

The name "Signifying Monkey" shows him to be a trickster, "signifying" being the language of trickery, that set of words or gestures which arrives at "direction through indirection" and which is used often to humiliate an adversary, especially among the young. It is a common device used by Negro children, but it is cause for reproach from their mothers. Indeed, there is a proverb often invoked against the user of this method, "Signifying is worse than dying."

The monkey, using this device of the child, is shown to be invoking his powers in an attempt to stir up trouble. And the dialogue that ensues shows how the process of signifying finds expression. The monkey is a master of the technique. Without any known provocation the monkey involves the lion in a fight with the elephant:

> Now the lion come through the jungle one peaceful day,
> When the signifying monkey stopped him and this is
>   what he started to say.
> He said, "Mr. Lion," he said, "A bad old so and so
>   down your way,"

> He said, "Yeah, the way he talks about your folks is
>   a certain shame.
> I even heard him curse when he mentioned your grandmother's
>   name."
> The lion's tail shot back like a forty-four
> When he went down that jungle in all uproar.

The struggle that ensues between the lion and the elephant is almost epic. The lion gets badly beaten, as could be expected. (At least the monkey expected it.) The monkey proceeds as a signifier to rub salt in his wounds from the safety of his tree.

> When they was fussing and fighting, lion come back
>   through the jungle more dead than alive,
> When the monkey started more of that signifying jive.
> He said, "Damn, Mr. Lion, you went through here
>   yesterday, the jungle rung.
> Now you come back today, damn near hung."

But the monkey's words are larger than his potential actions. His signifying leads him to get excited and he falls and is captured by the lion. He has to use all of his guile to escape from this situation, first calling on the sympathy and then on the pride of the lion:

> The monkey looked up with a tear in his eyes.
> He said, "Please Mr. Lion, I apologize."
> He said, "You lemme get my head out the sand,
> I'll fight you like a natural man."
> The lion jumped back and squared for a fight.
> The monkey jumped clear out of sight.

Once again he gets too excited while signifying from his tree-retreat and this time the lion has captured him for good.

> Again he started getting panicked and jumping up and down.
> His feet slipped and his back hit the ground.
> Like a bolt of lightning, stripe of white heat,
> Once more the lion was on the monkey with all four feet.
> Monkey looked up again with tears in his eyes.
> He said, "Please, Mr. Lion, I apologize."

Lion said, "Ain't gonna be no apologizing.
I'ma put an end to his signifying."
Now when you go through the jungle, there's a tombstone
  so they say,
"Here the Signifying Monkey lay."

So the unusual situation occurs where the hero dies. This fact seems significant. The trickster, as we have noted, is the eternal child. The Negro trickster story had a real place in the ante-bellum and post-bellum South where this was the sort of pose which the Negro was forced to assume; the subservient childlike creature, the "Uncle Tom" who was allowed his few tricks as his idiosyncracies. But the attitudes and values inherent in this approach to revolt have changed considerably. Because of recent developments in the lot of the Negro, especially in the northern cities, he has been able to express himself more overtly, and thus to escape his image as a perpetual child. Thus, it is not surprising that the trickster finds as little place as he does in the folklore of this group of Negro city-dwellers, and when he does exist in their traditional lore, his maneuvers often lead him not to triumph but to death.

Illustrative of this tendency away from trickster values is the change which comes over Brother Rabbit in the imaginations of these urbanites. The little animal becomes the strong man. The only story which I was able to collect of the ex-trickster includes the following description (Bear and Buzzard have tried to trick Rabbit into giving himself up by throwing a party and not inviting him):

Brother Rabbit was sitting on his post and all. Said, "Where you all going?" "Down to Brother Buzzard's house." "Brother Buzzard?" "Yeah, Brother Fox is giving a party over there." Rabbit ran to the house and got dressed and ran down to the house. Brother Buzzard said, "Sorry, Brother Rabbit, Brother Fox and Brother Bear say they don't want you in it. I'm sorry. That's what they told me."

So the rabbit turned away with his head turned down. He feeling sad, downhearted, tears in his eyes. Felt like he was alone in the world. But then he got mad. He said, "I know what I'll do." He went home and shined his shoes and got his shotgun and went back and kicked the door open. "Don't a man move." He walked over the table, got all he wanted to eat, walked over to the bar and got himself all he wanted to drink. He reached over and grabbed the Lion's wife and he danced with her. Grabbed the Ape's wife and did it to her. Then he walked out.

Agility is an attribute much more acceptable than guile. In his role as the great pool and card player the monkey finds greater success, as is seen in the toast of "The Monkey and the Baboon." In this tale the hero is portrayed as an adept at games and his agility pays off, for in this role he has acquired status symbols in his "smart" manner and his sharp clothes.

> Now a few stalks shook and a few leaves fell,
> And up jumped the monkey, sharp as hell.
> Had a one-button roll, two-button satch.
> You know, one of them boolhipper coats with a belt in the back.

The monkey still has power with his words, but he uses it simply to add a brilliant finish to the veneer of his actions. For instance, he is not satisfied to win at a game of cooncan; he must cap the game by laying down his cards in the following flourish of victory:

> So hop Mr. Rabbit and skip Mr. Bear.
> It's gonna look mighty shady but there's
>   'leven of them there.
> (A lay of eleven cards wins the game.)

But agility is not the ultimate in values to the Negro male; it is meanness, strength, and the ability to revolt in the face of authority and possible death. In this realm the badman reigns. He will often say such things as, "I'm a bad man and I don't mind dying." He is highly conscious of his role. The most characteristic and exciting of the badmen is "Stackolee."

"Stack" is a mean man, a purveyor of violence. He does not hesitate to hurt, taunt, kill, if someone offers him the slightest insult or reaction. Any act he does is executed with the greatest show of strength and arrogance, and with the smartest kind of flourish. Even though he is down on his luck when we first meet him, he doesn't let that affect his pride. Perhaps it serves to make him even more mean and deadly.

> I walked through water and I waded through mud.
> I came to a little-old hole in the wall called
>   "The Bucket of Blood."
> I walked in, asked the man for something to eat.
> Do you know that bastard gave me a stale glass
>   of water and a messed-up piece of meat.
> I said, "Raise up, man, do you know who I am?"
> He said, "Frankly, I don't give a damn."
> I knowed right then that sucker was dead.
> I throwed a thirty-eight shell through his head.

A girl comes over and offers herself in an obvious attempt to keep him there until the murdered man's brother Benny Long (or Billy Lyons) gets there. He accepts both challenges and wins them in the grandest of styles. He is as magnificent in sex as he is in battle. The two of them, upstairs, hear the door close below and know it is Benny Long.

> "But I'ma give you a chance my brother never got. I'ma
>   give you a chance to run,
> 'Fore I reach in my cashmere and pull out my gun."
> Just then some old sucker over in the corner said,
>   "Somebody call the law."
> He stretched out and put a forty-five shell through
>   that guy's jaw.
> A cute little broad came and said, "Benny, please."
> He blowed that broad down to her knees.
> And out went the lights.
> And Benny Long was in both of my thirty-eight sights.
> Now the lights came on and all the best,
> I sent that sucker to eternal rest,
> With thirteen thirty-eight bullet holes 'cross his chest.

Benny, as you see, is constructed just as mean and strong as Stack, so that Stack's triumph will be a fitting one. An

appropriate end to a story of this sort is the violent boast
delivered by Stack:

> I was raised in the backwoods, where my pa raised a bear.
> And I got three sets of jawbone teeth, and an extra layer of hair.
> When I was three I sat in a barrel of knives,
> Then a rattlesnake bit me, crawled off and died.
> So when I come in here, I'm no stranger.
> 'Cause when I leave, my footprint leaves "danger."

In such characters as Stackolee we have the embodiment
of the values of the community, especially those of the young
men. Such values, when acted upon, serve as a reminder of
masculinity to those doing the act, and to those vicariously
enjoying it. Such violent actions are the rebellion against
authority one expects in adolescents and others with an
adolescent ego development. The Negro male must find some
manner in which he can achieve self-respect, and this seems
to be the easiest way to express it within the confines of this
lower-class, semiliterate community.

In one story, the saga of the Negro stoker "Shine" aboard
the *Titanic* at the time of its sinking, we can begin to glimpse
some emergent values that differ to some degree from those
we have observed above. Briefly, the story is that Shine is the
one who informs the captain of the ship about the holes in
the hull after the crash of the ship with the iceberg. The
captain keeps sending him down to pump, and he keeps
re-emerging, giving the captain further information on the
size of the hole. Finally, Shine jumps in the water and begins
swimming, and he does so very well. He is then offered three
temptations from those still on board—money from the captain,
and sex from the captain's wife and his daughter. All of these
he turns down in favor of practicality. He is then challenged
by the shark and the whale but is able to outperform them.
He swims safely to the shore.

In Shine we have a hero who has guile and a trickster's

command of the language, but he is no trickster. We have a hero who has amazing physical powers, but he is much more than a badman or even a contest hero. He is able to perform acts which qualify him as a much more complete hero than any of the others we have encountered previously. First of all, he performs feats, is a "legendary hero." Shine's amazing action of swimming away from the sinking, even in outswimming the creatures whose natural habitat he has entered, qualifies him firmly as a performer of feats. Further, his declining of the temptations of money and sex add other attributes to his status as hero; he is a passer of trials, of tests.

Shine exhibits in his actions a sense of task which is conspicuously absent in the actions of any of the other heroes we have discussed. Stackolee, presented with a similar situation, would certainly have accepted the offer of sex and stolen the money. But Shine seems to perceive a direction to his actions. His abilities not only indicate an amazing physical and verbal talent but also show a capacity to turn his back on just those status symbols for which the other heroes have been fighting. After all, Stack and the Monkey are reacting against the insecurity caused by their poor financial state and their inability to express firmly their masculinity. But these are exactly those things which Shine is turning down in his replies to the captain, his wife, and his daughter. He would not be able to do so were not his sense of himself as an individual in a firmer state than we perceive in the other heroes of this group.

Shine makes it very clear that he is turning his back on white people. He answers one of the offers of the captain's wife:

> You know my color and you guessed my race.
> You better jump in the water and give these sharks a chase.

It is also clear throughout that his triumph is achieved in the name of his race. He is pointed out as a Negro on a ship that was renowned for not allowing that race aboard as passengers. He was thus isolated, away from his people, being tested. Do we not then have in this "toast" a message of some sociological and psychological significance? For here is a Negro story which overtly pictures his enemies as white. And the white man has been his authority figure against whom he has been rebelling. But here he achieves that greater act of rebellion, the turning of his back. This is then something of a declaration of independence.

We have then three different conceptions of the hero among these young Negroes. Yet there is one aspect that unites them: All are protest heroes, and all of them exhibit their reaction in comic, joking terms. This is, of course, appropriate in a situation of this sort. The joker hero is no less a redeemer than any other. He simply brings about his vivification through comedy and derision rather than through catharsis. This is because comedy is a social matter, tragedy more of an individual one. Furthermore, as Wylie Sypher says: "The comic perspective can be reached only by making game of 'serious' life. The comic rites are necessarily impious, for comedy is sacrilege as well as release."[13] The joker is the fool in modern guise, because through his banter he is exhibiting the divine efficacy of the questioner. He questions (by jokes as well as actions) at the same time as he exhibits and teaches. He punctures absurdities as inequities.

Once again, it is Shine's questioning that transcends the limitations of the inherent questions of the Monkey and Stack. Stack's comic approach is to show the absurdity of white man's morality by his brutality, almost a reversion when looked upon in civilization's terms. Shine, on the other hand, rises above this, questioning white man's values by laughing in his face and causing, through his quips, others to laugh, and, psychologically and physically, providing for himself.

However, we must resist trying to make too much out of this one story. It is, in the first place, atypical. Secondly, the tone of the story is pronouncedly defiant in a chest-pounding way, and the note on which it ends is a derisive joke:

> When news got to Washington that the
>   great Titanic had sunk
> Shine was standing on the corner
>   already one-half drunk.

Along with this toast of overt rebellion have come a number of other stories that are also openly reacting against the white's actions of dominance. Competition between Negro and white on the narrative level has emerged from the trickster and tricked level to one in which the terms and ideas are much less veiled.

In the narrative,[14] then, we see much the same struggle that can be noticed in the sociological and historical backgrounds of the urban Negro. And through the narrative we can begin to see the same great shift of emphasis which if broadened could have significant implications for the folklore of the Negro.

1. Such a device as the "signature" is strong evidence for this. At the end of a piece it returns the audience fully into the hands of the narrator and reminds them that he has been the motion behind the piece all along. For instance, one version of "The Monkey and the Baboon" uses this stock signature:

> If anybody asks you who pulled that toast,
> Just tell them old bullroaring Snell, from coast-to-coast,
> I live on Shotgun Avenue, Tommygun Drive
> Pistol Apartment, Room 45.

2. Richard Dorson seems to agree with this point of view. "Influenced by Harris . . . subsequent collections emphasized animal tales." *American Folklore* (Chicago, 1959), p. 176.

3. Richard Dorson's published collections offer the best cross-section of recent Negro tales, including important stories of the type listed here.

4. Orrin E. Clapp, "The Folk Hero," *Journal of American Folklore*, LXII (1949), 20.

5. Karl Kerényi, "The Trickster in Relation to Greek Mythology," Paul Radin, *The Trickster* (New York, 1956), p. 185. Kerényi goes on, commenting on the release mechanism of the trickster story: "Disorder belongs to the totality of life, and the spirit of this disorder is the trickster. . . . the function of his mythology, of the tales told about him, is to add disorder to order and so make a whole, to render possible, within the

fixed bounds of what is permitted, an experience of what is not permitted."

6. C. G. Jung, "On the Psychology of the Trickster Figure," in Radin, *op. cit.*, p. 203.

7. *Ibid.*, p. 211.

8. This identity of child and trickster seems to have been recognized early, as trickster festivals mocking the church or government in the Middle Ages, called among other things *festum puerorum. Ibid.*, p. 198.

9. The badman, as the trickster, channels destructive impulses into a formal unity.

10. "Trickster" in *The Standard Dictionary of Folklore, Mythology and Legend* (New York, 1949), p. 1123.

11. Jung, *op. cit.*, p. 203.

12. Clapp, *op. cit.*, p. 19.

13. Wylie Sypher, "The Meanings of Comedy," in *Comedy*, Essays by George Meredith and Henri Bergson (New York, 1956), p. 223.

14. Full texts of the narratives referred to in this paper, as well as other pertinent narratives, may be found in the author's unpublished dissertation, University of Pennsylvania, 1962.

Don Juan Zurumbete

RILEY AIKEN

This version of "The Brave Tailor" (tale type 1640) was secured from a countryman in the Rio Grande Valley near Palares, Mexico.

THIS WAS a fellow who was without depth in everything except the cup. He was a misfit and drifter, and his very lack of character was his character. It was said that the only thing he ever did right was the wrong thing. Once a young friend took him to task and said:

"Listen to me, Juan. You are on your way down and out. Get hold of yourself before it is too late. Remember the old saying:

> Agua que va río abajo
> Arriba no ha de volver."

To this Juan replied with affected solemnity: "Your intentions are good, *amiguito,* but surely you haven't forgotten what is said of good intentions. Furthermore, *amigo de mi alma,* my life is *muy mía* and is of more import to me than to you. You commune with an arbitrary principle and I with a bottle. *Y qué!* So what! And as for the waters of a river once downstream being downstream forever, my answer is: *A otro perro con ese hueso.*"

And the friends went their respective ways, one to a temple and the other to the nearest saloon.

Now, as the story begins, we find our sinner dead drunk,

135

bedded down by the side of a flea-bitten dog in the shadow of the walls of a run-down cantina. Juan could not sleep well. He saw rats everywhere; rats, *unas pintas y otras pardas*. He remembered the counsel of his friend and began to weep and then to laugh. He became aware of his bedmate and laughed louder.

"Yes," he said, "*mi vida es muy mía. Y qué!*"

A sad violin from somewhere in the dull distance began musing in fond memories of better days when men were men.

"What is life?" asked Juan, as he noted the behavior of seven flies that had come to rest on the back of his hand.

"Listen, *moscas*, I ask you, since you get around: What is life? What? You no speak? I'll show you what it is by what it isn't. *Zas!* Now you are seven dead flies, see, and I . . . I am a hero!"

Then Juan, moved by a festive impulse, took from his shirt pocket a small pencil and a piece of paper and wrote the following legend:

> Don Juan Zurumbete
> Que de un moquete
> Mató siete.

And this he stuck on the crown of his sombrero and went to sleep.

He was not long asleep when one of the king's emissaries happened by the cantina and saw the stranger and the legend on the sombrero.

"How curious!" he said. "How curious! And perhaps he is what the paper says. This could be an unusual man, for there are few since the days of Bernardo del Carpo who with one stroke of the hand can kill seven men. Yes, my king must know about this. We need such a hero to fight the Moors for us. I shall go tell him that I have found a champion in this cantina who calls himself Don Juan Zurumbete, who, with one slap of the hand, killed seven men."

Soon the emissary stood before the king and related to him his discovery.

"Fool!" said the king. "Why return to me without this warrior? Go immediately and get him. We can use such a man in our war with the Moors."

The emissary went immediately to the cantina and woke Juan Zurumbete.

"Get up!" he commanded. "Get up, and come with me to the king."

"And what if I don't want to speak to the king?" asked Juan. "If he wants to speak to me, *ésta es su casa.*"

The emissary was amazed at such audacity but dared not say another word for was this not

> Don Juan Zurumbete
> Que de un moquete
> Mató siete?

He returned to His Majesty.

"Where is our man?" asked the king. "Why did you return without him?"

"Because, Your Majesty, I dared not try to compel a man who has killed seven with one blow of the hand," said the emissary. "It seems, Your Majesty, this is a situation demanding discretion. Would it not be wiser to devise some milder means for bringing this great warrior to your castle?"

The king was impressed. "Yes, you may be right," said the king. "Go tell him I invite him to a banquet."

The emissary brought this message to Juan.

"Why does he want me at his banquet?" asked Juan.

"Because we know who you are," answered the emissary. "We know you are a great warrior who has killed seven men with one stroke of the hand. If that is not true, then why the legend on your hat?"

Juan laughed and was about to explain, when suddenly he decided to play along with the king's wish.

Juan met the king and said that indeed he had once killed seven with one stroke of the hand.

"That is the reason we hold you in high esteem," said the king. "We are at war with the Moors, and are now, because of the death of my son, at the point of defeat. You are our last hope. If you will serve me faithfully and successfully, I shall give you my daughter in marriage."

Juan, a coward by nature, decided to admit the deception he had practiced. But again, he was prompted to accept the role of hero.

"There is nothing to do," he told himself, "but entrust myself to fate. If by chance I have an early opportunity to leave this kingdom, I shall go."

Don Juan Zurumbete was dined, feted, and wined and on the following morning he was placed astride the famous war-horse of the dead prince. Hardly was he in the stirrups before the horse was off toward the rising sun.

Now just a few days before the king's only son had been slain by the Moors, and this famous horse was burning to avenge the death of his master. There was no steed in the whole kingdom that knew more ways of killing the enemy than he.

Miles flew by and presently Don Juan saw a lazy smoke in a valley below.

"The Moors!" he thought. "*Madre mía,* now what am I to do?"

The Moors had mounted for their morning drill when they saw the lone horseman coming with furious speed from the west. They had never seen such daring, and they turned to flee. One by one they were run down by the famous horse and killed.

Great was the reception at the castle. Don Juan Zurumbete was not only a hero who had killed seven men with one stroke of the hand, but now the champion of a kingdom who had run down and slain a whole army of Moors.

In the meantime Don Juan had seen the princess. She was more beautiful than the sun, moon, and stars. Although completely lacking in moral fortitude, he could not refrain from asking for her hand in marriage. The king, however, had begun to suspect that Don Juan was an impostor. Yet he could not resist the fact that he was

> Don Juan Zurumbete
> Que de un moquete
> Mató siete,

and who had annihilated the Moors, his enemies. He made excuses for postponing an early marriage and devised a scheme for the riddance of Don Juan.

It seemed, according to the king, that for some years two giants had been terrorizing the land. Don Juan was assigned the task of killing them.

"Válgame Dios," he said, "is there no end to my troubles? True, a horse saved me with the Moors, but only fate can help me now."

He mounted his famous horse and rode away. After some days he came to the region of the giants. Don Juan had dismounted to cinch his saddle when one of the mountain men came upon him. The horse broke for safety. Don Juan took to timber and crawled into a hollow tree. The giants roared about in search of their prey. At last they found him, and feeling he would be better eating roasted, they pulled up the tree by its roots and proceeded to carry it on their shoulders to their camp.

It was now very dark. Don Juan in desperation decided on aggression. He crawled along the log which was being carried on the shoulders of the two giants as they trailed through the forest. When he reached the one in the lead he hit him on the ear with his fist. Turning, the offended one yelled:

"Why are you hitting me, fool? I have the heavier end to carry. Attend to your end of the trunk and let me be!"

Then, turning toward the other end, Don Juan struck the second monster on the ear.

"So you want to fight!" yelled this monster. "Well, let me tell you something. You are a coward and a liar!"

After a bit Don Juan, having as before proceeded along the trunk to the leader, struck him a blow with a dead limb.

"This is too much!" said the giant. "*Ahora verás!*"

They threw their load to the ground and fought until they had torn each other to small bits.

Don Juan gathered up four ears from the ground and returned to the king's castle.

"There is one other request I have to make," said the king. "A monstrous serpent has been killing shepherds and their flocks in a valley of my kingdom. Kill this monster and you may marry my daughter. This I promise by my word as king."

No sooner was Don Juan Zurumbete in the valley of the serpent than the latter spied him and gave chase. Don Juan hit for the mountains with the speed of the wind, and went scrambling up a peak. He climbed with such desperation that he set the boulders rolling. One of these, a large one, headed straight for the serpent. It landed in the monster's mouth, killed him, and rolled with him into the valley below.

Don Juan, after gathering his wits, climbed down the peak, picked up a serpent fang as long as a man's arm, and made his way back to the castle.

The people hailed him as the greatest hero of all ages. He married the king's daughter and built himself a castle larger than that of the king. And the latter was afraid to do anything about it, for wasn't his son-in-law

> Don Juan Zurumbete
> Que de un moquete
> Mató siete?

Work and Play on a Border Ranch

ROSALINDA GONZALEZ

IT IS HARD for us to imagine the old days along the Border between the Lower Rio Grande Valley and Mexico; but it takes a few old-timers just a little while to bring it alive to us. If one has a relative who has lived in the Valley for fifty years or more, he is lucky indeed, for such a person may serve as a means of gaining better understanding of the culture that has evolved along the Border.

One hundred and fifty years ago, the ranch settlements along the Rio Grande were permeated by the Old Spanish and Mexican customs and traditions. They could be found in the language, the food, the homes, the social life of young and old, and the kind of work done on the ranches.

One particular ranch, fondly called La Esperanza by its inhabitants, was a typical example of this. Its activities have been brought alive to me through the years by my parents and relatives, especially by my mother, who has lived in the Valley for fifty years, and by my maternal grandfather, who has lived there for eighty-three years.

My mother was born in Run, a small ranch several miles from La Esperanza. Run was a part of the bigger La Blanca Ranch where her father was born. She went to live at La Esperanza in 1910 when she was just a year old, and she spent eight years of her childhood there. Nor was her contact with the ranch broken in her later life, for she returned there for short stays many times.

The original La Esperanza Ranch extended east to west from Val Verde to Alamo Road, as far north as the eighteen-mile line near Edinburg, and as far south as the edge of the Rio Grande. When it was first bought, it contained 3,330 acres; by 1910, when my mother went to live there, it had only about 200 acres.

The ranch was owned by my maternal great-grandfather, who bought it around 1880 from Juan J. Trevino. It may have been one of the four grants made by the Mexican government in 1834, for a Juan Jose Trevino is named as having been given the Agostadero del Gato Grant,[1] and my mother remembers being told that the ranch was on the Agostadero del Gato Grant. My grandfather also mentioned an El Gato Ranch as being the ranch where his father kept a good herd of horses in corrals.

The La Blanca Ranch, where my grandfather was born, was to the east of La Esperanza Ranch. It also may have been part of a grant given by the Mexican government in 1834, for the Mexican La Blanca Grant was the site of present-day Donna,[2] the town which my grandfather said was previously the territory of his father's ranch. The La Blanca Grant was first given to Lino Cavazos,[3] a person whom my mother remembers as having been mentioned by her mother. He may be an ancestor, too, for my maternal grandfather's father was a Cavazos.

I first visited the ranch in the early forties. The few relatives who had remained there still lived in part-sod, part-lumber houses without modern conveniences. Though their homes were old-fashioned, their work showed a change from the old days. They engaged more in crop-raising than in stock-raising, the main occupation of the people at the time my great-grandparents and grandparents lived there. Today, a few distant relatives still live in the area covered by the old ranch. Most of the land is divided by the military highway and is being farmed. A few mesquites and a few gravestones are the only reminders of the old rancho to be found today.

Stock-raising was very important at La Esperanza Ranch, each family having its herd of cattle, sheep, goats, hogs, and horses. The care of these animals was mainly in the hands of the men; but the women helped with some of the chores. For example, my second cousin told me that her mother (a niece of my grandfather) used to get up at four-thirty in the morning to milk the cows.

Because the ranch was in what is called a "monte"—brush country—it needed to be self-sufficient; and it almost was, as were most ranches in those days. With all the livestock to provide them with food and with all the food crops raised on the ranch land, the people were pretty well off. They had to depend on their land and cattle, for there were no modern cities they could rush to when they wanted necessities. The fact that the people on the ranch were related helped them to be more independent, because the sharing of the work led to better living conditions.

As important as stock-raising on the ranch was the raising of crops. About fifty acres of land at the ranch was put in cultivation for corn, watermelons, pink beans, Mexican pumpkins, and cotton.

One minor activity was beekeeping, an occupation of Mexican natives since before the conquest of Cortez.[4] The beehives were kept under a row of elm, hackberry, and "tepequaje"[5] trees. From the hives would come four or five tubfuls of combs, which were squeezed in a cloth, with a person on each side rolling the ends over to squeeze the honey out. In this manner they got the honey to deposit in barrels and glass jars. My mother remembers that two barrels of about fifty-gallon capacity were always filled with honey.

A day at the ranch started very early—around four-thirty or five in the morning. At this time, the cows and goats were milked and the cattle, sheep, and horses were taken to pasture. The women would get up to fix the fire and to prepare coffee to give to the men before they set out to do these chores.

Usually there was no time for idleness. Water for the animals and for home use had to be gotten from a sixty-foot well on the ranch; the goats and sheep had to be looked after; the land had to be plowed and planted; and the crops had to be harvested. Then the hogs had to be killed for their lard and meat and the sheep had to be sheared for their wool.

The work of the women was also endless. They cooked meals; prepared the meats; made clothes and quilts; helped kill and clean the hogs, sheep, and chickens. Along with this they made their own soap, cheese, and butter.

The meat at the ranch came not only from the ranch animals, but from the deer that roamed in the brush and mesquite of the ranch. My mother says it was her father's delight to hunt the deer. Many are the tales that he can tell you of his hunting trips. Although eighty-three years of age, he recalls many of those trips vividly and seems to relive them. According to my mother, he also liked to hunt at night with traps. He would catch raccoons, skunks, coyotes, and foxes, and would take wagonloads of their fur and hides to sell in Brownsville.

My mother told me of a quaint custom my grandfather used to observe in the cornfields. In the morning, alone or sometimes with my grandmother, he would take a picture of San Isidro to the fields and parade it through the rows of corn. Then he would hang it somewhere while he went about his work. In the evening he would take it home. This was usually done when it was too dry and when the corn was in need of water. As he paraded the picture of San Isidro, he would recite a little prayer:

San Isidro, labrador,	Saint Isidro, farmer,
San Isidro, labrador,	Saint Isidro, farmer,
Quita el sol y pon	Take away the sun and
el agua.	bring the rain.

When it rained too much, the little prayer would change to a request for the opposite:

San Isidro, labrador,
San Isidro, labrador,
Quita el agua y pon
     el sol.

Saint Isidro, farmer,
Saint Isidro, farmer,
Take away the rain and
     bring back the sun.

I had never heard of this custom before; but I have since found that it stems from the Catholic customs connected with farming in Mexico.

My mother says that the others at the ranch knew of this practice but did not observe it, although they would have liked to. Grandfather's brother-in-law was one of these. His land was next to Grandfather's, and once he told Grandfather that he had thought of parading San Isidro in his field, too, but reasoned that if it rained in Grandfather's field, it would rain in his also. Grandfather admonished him, telling him that he should at least say the prayers with him so that it would rain.

Religion has played an important part in the farming customs of Mexico; and my grandfather's observance of this custom indicates that religion has also influenced the people on this side of the Border.

Another example of this religious influence on farming customs, even in modern times, is the following incident. About eleven years ago, my mother noticed at her first cousin's home a stem of cotton with open cotton boll arched over a picture of a saint. When my mother asked her why she had arranged the cotton stem like that, her cousin replied that she had offered it to the saint in order that he would give them a good crop.

Despite constant work, life was not dull around the ranch. For the children there was play in endless variety, and for the elders there were an endless number of tales, stories, and riddles. Today many of the songs, games, riddles, sayings, beliefs, and superstitions formerly prevalent at the ranch are heard of only occasionally.

Playing with dolls was a pastime enjoyed by the little ranch girls. Since "store-bought" dolls were few, they made their little dolls with rags; and like little girls of today, they also made the clothes for them. Boxes were fixed with little beds for the dolls and were used while they played "Las Comadritas,"[6] a game in which they visited each other and talked about their little "children." The yellow, fuzzy flowers of the mesquites were used for "food" to serve the "comadre" who came visiting.

Even the eggs of the birds were used in girls' play. During the summer, they would climb into the mesquite, hackberry, and huisache trees in search of birds' eggs. Only one was taken from each nest so "the mother bird would not get angry." Taking home their loot, the little girls would fashion new nests for the eggs out of shucks of corn.

The young boys did not have as much opportunity to play as did the little girls. This was especially true during the time my mother was at the ranch; but her mother used to tell her that at the school at Run, where she met my grandfather, the boys played baseball with a ball made of rags. Generally the boys played alone; but sometimes they allowed the girls to play with them. The players had their own rules. They used three bases, not four. Instead of running with the ball to put someone out, they threw the ball at the runner.

Mother described to me a religious game that was played at the ranch and at the Catholic school in Donna in the early twenties. It is similar to "Old Uncle Tom," a game that came to Texas from the eastern and southern parts of the United States.[7] It has no set name that I could place, but it could be called the "Color Game." I remember this game fondly myself, for as a young girl I used to play it. The game, which is played inside a room, requires many players. Two persons, captains, choose the ones they would like on their team; and they give each one the name of a certain color. This is done while two other persons, one playing the Angel and the other the Devil, are outside waiting to come in. The Angel and the Devil decide among themselves as to who will be the first to enter. Whoever gets the first chance (in this case, the Devil) knocks and one of the captains asks: "Who is it?"

"I'm the Devil."

"What do you want?"

"A color."

"What color?"

The Devil, let into the room, indicates the color he wants and the person representing that color has to go with him. It is in this manner that the Devil and the Angel claim their own. However, before letting the person go, the captain would request the Devil to do something for him. The fun of the game was to see whose choice you would be, and also to see what the captain would demand, for the demands could be hilarious.

Two requests that sent a group into gales of laughter during a game were the ones made by the teacher of the Catholic school. They lose almost all their meaning and charm when translated into English, but I will attempt to explain why they were so amusing. According to my mother, the saying that pertained to her was the following: "Llévesela, pero siéntemela en una piedra liza porque es hija de Doña Eloisa." "Take her, but sit her on a polished rock because she is the daughter of Lady Eloisa." The element of laughter in this is the rhyming of "piedra liza" with the name "Doña Eloisa." For my aunt, the saying went like this: "Llévesela, pero no me la siente en un tonel porque es hija de Don Daniel." "Take her, but do not sit her on a ton because she is the daughter of Mister Daniel." The laughter-provoking words are "tonel" and "Don Daniel." The fact that the teacher was able to find words to rhyme with the names of my mother's and aunt's parents also brought laughter.

Another game that was played at the ranch—one I remember playing, too—is "La Puerta Está Quebrada" (The Door Is Broken). This game is played like the English game, "London Bridge Is Falling Down." Two persons, each representing some object (sometimes an orange and a grapefruit) would make an arch with their hands. As the persons in the game went under the arch, they would sing:

La puerta está quebrada	The door is broken
Ya la van a componer.	It is going to be fixed.
Él que pase ha de pasar,	He who wants to pass should pass
Y él que no se ha de quedar.	And he who does not want to pass
	shall stay behind.

The following verse that the Mexican children sing to this game was used as part of the above by the ranch children.[8]

A la víbora, víbora	To the serpent, the serpent
De la mar, de la mar	Of the sea, of the sea,
Por aquí pueden pasar.	Here it can pass by.
La de adelante corre mucho	The one in front runs fast
La de atras se quedara ...	The one in back will remain
Tras, tras, tras, tras.	Behind, behind, behind, behind.

At the end of the words of the verse, the orange and the grapefruit would lower their arms to catch whoever was passing through at that time. The person caught would then be taken aside and asked in whispers (so that the others would not hear what objects they represented) whether he wanted the orange or the grapefruit. If he chose the orange he would stay behind the person playing the orange, while the other rounds through the arch were made to catch more of the players. By the time everyone was caught, each leader would have enough on his side to have a tug-of-war to see who would win the game. Of course, out of preference, one of the leaders would generally have more on his side.

"María Blanca" was another game that was known at the ranch, but it was not played much because the older girls did not care to play it with my mother and the other younger children. It is also a familiar game to me because I used to play it at home and at school. The children of Mexico play this game, but they call it "Doña Blanca" (The White Lady), according to Frances Toor's description in her *A Treasury of Mexican Folkways*.[9] The game was learned at the Donna Catholic school after the teacher had brought it from Penitas. They played it somewhat as the Mexican children do, although my mother does not remember whether they used the last two little verses of the game that the Mexican children use.

The children form a circle holding hands. In the center is a girl, Doña Blanca; outside, a boy who is Jicotillo, the hornet. All sing:

Doña Blanca está cubierta	The White Lady is covered
Con pilares de oro y plata	With pillars of gold and silver
Rómperemos un pilar	Let us break down a pillar
Para ver a Doña Blanca.	To see the White Lady.

Then the circle moves to the right and Doña Blanca sings:

Quién es ese Jicotillo	Who is that Jicotillo
Que anda rondando mi casa?	Hovering around my house?

The boy outside, Jicotillo, answers:

Yo soy, yo soy ese	I am that one, I am that one,
Que anda en pos de Doña Blanca.	Who is after Doña Blanca.

The pillars are broken with the children letting go of each other's hands. Jicotillo runs after Doña Blanca; when he catches her she forfeits her role, and the game continues with another girl playing María Blanca.

Another game of those days was the "Naranja Dulce, Limón Partido" game. It is another of the games of the Mexican children that Frances Toor describes.[10] The children form a circle with a person in the center. Miss Toor does not indicate what the children do as they sing the verse of the game; but according to my mother, they are supposed to move around the person in the center, who is also turning to see whom she would like to choose for the demand of the song. The song goes like this:

Naranja dulce, limón partido	Sweet orange, divided lemon,
Dame un abrazo que yo te pido;	Give me an embrace, I beg you;
Si fueran falsos mis juramentos,	If my vows were false
In otros tiempos se olvidarán.	In time they will be forgotten.
Toca la marcha, mi pecho llora	Play the march, my heart weeps;
Adiós, Señora, yo ya me voy.	Goodbye, Señora, I go now.

After the verse is finished, states Miss Toor, the one in the center approaches someone in the circle to comply with the request in the song and exchanges places with him. My mother and her friends played it a little bit differently. After the second line of the verse was sung, the person in the center would choose the one he wanted to embrace and would then kneel down on one knee and sing the rest of the song, and then change places with the one he had sung to.

I have heard my mother sing the song of this little game for as long as I can remember; but it was not until recently that I learned that it was part of a game.

Around Christmas time, especially on December 28, the Day of the Holy Innocents, which is Mexico's April Fool's Day,[11] the people at the ranch diverted themselves by playing tricks and saying the following little verse to the one who was fooled:

Inocente palomita,	Innocent little dove,
Que te dejaste engañar,	That let yourself be fooled
Sabiendo que en este día	Knowing that on this day
Nada se debe prestar.	Nothing should be lent.

A favorite trick in Mexico is to send these verses on a piece of paper with a silly toy in reply to a request for a loan of something.[12]

Another favorite pastime at the ranch, especially among the elders, was the telling of riddles. Within the riddles was a certain wisdom which the ranchers understood. According to my mother, these riddles, or *adividanzas*, always popped out at any gathering, large or small; but especially were they recited on Christmas and New Year's Day when the families would gather to eat tamales and other dishes. "Anyone could say them if they were smart enough to learn them from books that had them," she said. Grandfather said that the riddles were just handed down through the years, and that they could also be found in books. Recently I found a small booklet of riddles published in Mexico City. It seems that the Mexican people still enjoy themselves with them as did the people at the ranch long ago. The riddle about the ring, which is related later, was the only one familiar to me. But my mother had heard some of them said in other ways.

The following are some of the riddles that my grandfather has related to me:

Soy de cutise blanco	I am of white skin
De corazón negro	Of black heart
Que retorciones me hacen	Twistings are made on me
Que a veces me matan.	Sometimes they kill me.
Answer: A cigarette.	

Barbas coloradoas	Red beard
Rodillas para atras	Back-sided knees
Cara de cuerno	Face of horn
Tú lo seras.	Is what you are.
Answer: A rooster.	

Blanco fué mi nacimiento	White was my birth
Me pintaron de colores.	I was painted with colors.
He causado muchas muertes	I have caused many deaths
Y he enpobrecido senores.	And I have made men poor.
Answer: A deck of cards.	

Soy quien me miran nomás	I'm what you only see
Que todo lo mío doy	That everything of mine I give
Pero sin rascarme atras	But without scratching my back
Porque entonces nada soy.	Because then I'll be nothing.
Answer: A mirror.	

Tres pajaros en un palo	Three birds on a branch
Y tres hombres tirando	And three men shooting
Cada uno mató el suyo	Each one killed his
Y dos se fueron volando.	And two flew away.

Answer: "Cada uno" was the name of one man. He got his bird and the other two flew away.

From a niece of my grandfather came this one:

| Retorción, retorción | A turn, a turn |
| Cuida la casa como un león. | Guards the house like a lion. |

Answer: Key to a house.

From my mother came these two:

| Redondito, redondón | Round—very large or small |
| Que no tiene tapa ni tapón. | Has no cover or stopper. |

Answer: A ring.

| Patio barrido, patio regado | Swept patio, watered patio |
| Sale un viejito muy empinado. | Comes out an old, bent man. |

Answer: The *metate*.

The last riddle needs a little explanation. The *metate* is the kitchen utensil used by the Mexican people for grinding and rolling corn into corn meal for tortillas. As the women gather the corn meal or *masa*, they sweep it across the surface of the *metate* and as they sweep it across they carry along whatever milk has come out of the fresh corn, thus watering the *metate* as they sweep it with the meal. A *metate* does not have a level surface. One end is low while the other is tilted upward, making it look like an old, bent man.

A favorite *adividanza* of mine is the one about the hawk and the doves. I first heard it from my grandfather as a young child. It was one of the hardest riddles he ever gave us young children. He always ended up by giving us the answer— thirty-six; even recently, when he again related it to us, he had to supply the answer. I resorted to the modern way of calculation—algebra—to get the answer; but my grandfather's method is generally the same in theory. In Spanish the riddle goes like this:

Pasa un gavilán volando
Y viendo unas palomas en un ramo dice:
"Adiós, palomar de cien palomas!"
Oyéndolo le contesta el dueño:
"Con éstas, y otros tantas como éstas,
Y la mitad de éstas, y cuarta parte de
Éstas, y usted, Señor Gavilán, se completan
las cien palomas. Dime, ¿cuántas palomas son?"

Translated:

A hawk flies by
And seeing some doves on a branch he says:
"Goodbye, brood of one hundred doves!"
Hearing him, the owner answers:
"With these, and another as many as these, and one-half
Of these, and one-fourth of these, and you, Mister Hawk,
Make up the one hundred doves. Tell me, how many doves
are there?"

Dances and songs were no strangers to the ranch. In 1927, Mother's family returned to the ranch for five months to pick cotton. In the evening, the young men and girls would play records on an old victrola and would dance to the songs. The favorites were "El Hijo Pródigo" (The Prodigal Son); "El Abandodado" (The Abandoned One); "La Paloma" (The Dove); "La Casita" (The Little House); and "Adelita," a song which, says Miss Toor, was the most beloved of all revolutionary songs in Mexico.[13] Another favorite dance tune was "Valencia." The "Jarabe Tapatio," which developed around 1920, in Guadalajara, Jalisco, Mexico,[14] was played but none of the young people knew how to dance to it.

Sayings, beliefs, and superstitions made life on the ranch more interesting. A saying concerning marriage was, "Tomar agua en taza te casas con uno de la casa." (If one drank water from a cup, he would marry a relative.) "Mucho ruido y pocas nueces" (Much noise but few nuts)[15] was heard often at the ranch, according to my mother. Another common saying was, "No hay borracho que coma lumbre" (Not even a drunkard will eat fire).[16] Also familiar there was this one: "Si tu mal tiene remedio, para qué te apuras, y si no tiene, para qué te apuras?" (If your evil has a remedy, why fret yourself; if it does not, why fret?)[17]

The following saying was expressed by both my grandfather's father and my great-grandfather's wife: "Cuando el tecolote canta el indio muere. Ésto no sera verdad, pero sucede." (When the owl hoots, the Indian dies. This may not be true, but it happens.)[18]

It is not strange that the saying "Siempre la res busca el monte" (Cattle always seek the cover of the brush) was used at the ranch.

The broom figured in some beliefs and superstitions at the ranch. It was bad luck to sweep at night, but it was good luck to place the broom with the straw part uppermost. It was also bad luck to jump over a broom. If you did, you would have to rejump it in order to prevent bad luck. These superstitions are still prevalent in the lives of people of Mexican descent who live in the Valley. They have been common sayings in my home ever since I can remember. I have found that my friends have also known about them for a long time.

Ranch life in the old days in the Valley had its charm. It was a distinct way of life that has produced a hardy people of whom my mother and maternal grandfather are good examples. Such pioneers as they, who remember well how they lived and how they played, are the ones who help us recognize the fascination of the old days.

1. J. Lee and Lillian J. Stambaugh, *The Lower Rio Grande Valley of Texas* (San Antonio: Naylor, 1954), pp. 43-44.

2. Florence Johnson Scott, *Historical Heritage of the Lower Rio Grande Valley* (San Antonio: Naylor, 1937), p. 169.

3. Stambaugh, *op. cit.*, pp. 43-44.

4. Frances Toor, *A Treasury of Mexican Folkways* (New York: Crown, 1947), p. 24.

5. The "tepequaje" is a tree with very hard and compact wood. I have not been able to find the English name for this tree.

6. "Las Comadritas" is equivalent to the American game of "playing house" or "having tea." The little girls imitate their mothers' social life by visiting each other, talking about their "children" (the dolls), and offering their "comadre" (godmother of their child) a little something to eat and drink. Although "comadre" means "godmother," it is also used to denote a friend.

7. Ida B. Hall, "Pioneer Children's Games," in *Texian Stomping Grounds* ("Publications of the Texas Folklore Society," XVII [1941]), p. 145.

8. Toor, *op. cit.*, pp. 272-73.

9. *Ibid.*, pp. 269-70.

10. *Ibid.*, p. 271.

11. *Ibid.*, p. 250.

12. *Ibid.*

13. *Ibid.*, p. 411.

14. *Ibid.*, p. 364.

15. Also in *ibid.*, p. 541.

16. *Ibid.*

17. Also in Howard D. Wesley, "Ranchero Sayings of the Border," in *Puro Mexicano* ("Publications of the Texas Folklore Society," XII [1935]), p. 213.

18. Toor, *op. cit.*, p. 541.

Cuentos de Susto

BALDEMAR A. JIMÉNEZ

THE FOLLOWING stories are for the most part tales which I heard in Spanish as a young boy in San Antonio, Texas. I cannot remember the specific person, or persons, who told me these *cuentos,* but they soon became a part of me. Retelling them became one of my favorite pastimes.

In Spanish, these tales are known as *cuentos de susto,* which means stories dealing with fright. That is, the main purpose of this type of *cuento* is to frighten the listener. It was for this reason that most of the storytelling was carried on after dark.

At times the telling was so vivid that it caused some very interesting reactions in some of my playmates. There was one little girl who loved to listen to these tales, but was so emotional that she either fainted at the ending or had to be walked home. And there was a little boy whose eyes would fill with tears during the telling. We used to laugh at him, because he always claimed that he was not crying. He was among those who were always asking to hear the tales again.

The Three Daughters

In a little town very far away in Mexico, there lived a woman whose name was Doña María Gonzales. She had three daughters. The oldest was named Elvira, the middle Yolanda, and the youngest Rosita. The woman's husband, Genaro, worked all day out in the fields of the little farm they owned.

Doña María had spoiled all the three daughters very much. She did all the housework. She would do all the cooking, washing, and ironing. If she asked Rosita to dust the furniture, Rosita would say, "*Mamacita,* you do it, I am very busy playing with my dolls."

If she asked Yolanda to wash the dishes, Yolanda would answer, "*Mamacita,* you do it, I am very busy cleaning my fingernails. The water and soap would ruin them."

If she asked the oldest daughter to help her make the tortillas, she would answer, "*Mamacita,* you do it, I am very busy combing my hair."

The mother would always walk away shaking her head and saying, "*Pobrecitas, mis niñitas,* they are still so young; I can do it myself."

The neighbors would say to Doña María, "You should not spoil them so very much. When they get married and must keep their own home, they will not know how to do it. Or if something should happen to you before they marry, what will become of them?"

Doña María would always answer, "Nothing will happen to me while they need me. And besides, they are still too young to do anything."

The neighbors would talk to her husband. They would say, "Genaro, look at the way your wife spoils the girls. You should not let her. It is not right."

He would always smile and say, "My wife, she is so kind. She knows what she does in her own home."

One day, the mother started feeling sick. She kept on doing the housework, but she felt weaker and weaker as the days passed. At first the girls were too busy to notice how sick she was. Finally, they began to notice a sore on her throat which grew bigger every day. It kept right on growing until the mother had to cover it with a handkerchief. She tried all sorts of *remedios,* but none of them did her any good. She only grew worse. Now she tried to show her daughters how to apply themselves. But it was too late. IIer health got worse and worse very quickly, and she died.

Her husband and her daughters cried very much at her death. They missed her greatly now that she was dead. The husband tried very hard to keep his neighbors from burying his wife, but he knew that it must be done. They buried her on a little hill very near the house.

The daughters now had to do all the housework, but they were very clumsy. Rosita would sweep and leave dirt in every corner of the house. Yolanda would wash the dishes and cry because her fingernails broke. Elvira tried to make the tortillas, but she burned most of them. Then the father would say, "My daughters, you must do the housework much better than you are doing it." But they could not do any better for a long time.

After a while, they did learn to do certain things, but with great difficulty. They were learning to do a good job of cooking, washing, and cleaning the house. But no matter how much they cleaned the house, they could not get rid of a certain bad odor which had first become noticeable shortly after their mother's death.

At night, every shadow seemed alive. The girls heard mysterious and unnatural noises. Thirteen days after Doña María died, and every night thereafter, a ghost would appear in the girls' bedroom. It was in the form of a woman in a white gown with her hair hanging down loose over her shoulders.

When she appeared, she would motion with her hand at the girls, asking them to follow her. They would follow, and she would lead them into the living room. She would stand before the large closet in that room and then disappear. It was from the closet that the bad odor came. In the morning, they would tell their father what they had seen, but he would never let them open the closet to see what was in it or to clean it up.

One day, while they were busily cleaning the house and pouring perfumes near the closet to cover the bad odor, a man dressed in black came to their door. He said he was a traveler and that he was tired and hungry. He asked them if they would give him some water and food. They said they would, and he ate. When he was getting ready to leave, he gave each of them a present. He gave Elvira some perfume, Yolanda a hat and a fan, and Rosita a necklace. When he left, the girls were very scared.

Rosita said, "Did you see his eyes? They were glowing red like fire."

"Yes," said Yolanda, "but did you see his feet? They were like those of a horse."

"No, no," protested Rosita; "they were more like those of a rooster."

"You are both wrong," Elvira said; "his feet were like those of a monkey."

But since he had given them all presents, they agreed that he must not have been evil even if he was a spirit. They put away their gifts in a bureau next to the closet in the living room. When their father came in from the fields that evening, they did not tell him of the stranger. He would have been very angry if he had known that they had allowed a stranger to come into the house.

About a week later, when the bishop of the area came to their little town to visit the church, the girls decided to go to mass. They also decided to use the presents that the stranger had given them. They all went to the bureau. Rosita opened her drawer first and found that her necklace had changed into a snake. They threw the snake out the door and killed it. Then Yolanda opened her drawer and found that the hat and the fan had changed into a skull and some greenish bones. By this time Elvira was very much afraid to open the drawer in which she had placed her present. After a lot of urging by her sisters, she did open it and found that the beautiful-smelling perfume had turned into a foul-smelling, bloodlike liquid.

They were so scared that they ran all the way to church and told the bishop of all the things they had seen since their mother's death. He ordered a procession to be formed, and they all marched over to the house with the bishop and the girls in the lead. As they got closer to the house, the bishop started to pray aloud. They walked into the house, the bishop still praying. As the bishop stood before the closet, he sprinkled holy water before the locked door. Slowly, very slowly, it started to open and immediately there was a heavy, sulphurous odor. Then the door burst open with such force that it shook the whole house.

Everyone was horrified to see the sight before them. In the closet was the badly decomposed body of Doña María. It was now obvious that the deteriorated body was the cause of the bad odor.

The people wrapped the body up in several thick blankets and took it outside. Then they called Don Genaro from the fields, and he confessed that he had taken the body out of the grave. He said he could not stand to have his kind wife buried in the cold dirt where all the worms could get to her. He then told them of how he had applied wax over the body of his wife the first thirteen nights to keep it from decomposing. But lately, he said, a ghost had been appearing every night and waking up his daughters. This action had prevented him from applying any more wax; thus he explained the present condition of his wife.

The bishop told him that all the unrest in the house was caused by Doña María's suffering soul. He said that the only way to destroy the evil in the house was to rebury her. Only then would her wandering soul rest. On hearing the bishop say this, Don Genaro agreed that it was the best thing.

And from that day forth no other mysterious things happened to the family of Don Genaro Gonzales.

The Figs

This was a lady who had two children, a boy and a girl. Her husband went to work very early in the morning, and he did not come home until very late in the evening. She was always preparing special treats for him, because he came home very tired every day.

When her husband returned from his work, she would have a hot supper ready for him. After supper, she would bring out a freshly made pie, a cake, or some fresh fruit for him to eat. He always enjoyed these special treats very much after the long hours he spent at work. After such well-prepared dinners, he was very affectionate to his wife. They would talk about the things of the day. She was very happy to be able to talk to her husband.

One day, early in the morning, when she did not have any flour for making a pie or cake, she saw that the fig tree was full of figs. They were just right for eating. She decided that she would give her husband fresh figs that evening. She knew he would enjoy such a treat. She called Roberto and Rebecca, her little boy and her little girl, and told them to climb the tree and pick the very best figs for her.

In a short while, all the best figs had been picked off the tree by the children. Roberto and Rebecca climbed down from the tree. The mother said to them, "These figs are for your father. I don't want you to eat them, because they are all I have for his treat tonight." Both of the children promised that they would not eat the figs.

As the children went off to play in the backyard, the mother took the figs and set them on the window sill where they would keep fresh and cool. She went about doing her housework all day, and it was not until much later that she decided it was time to start preparing supper. She went to the window sill and found all the figs gone. She hurried out into the backyard. In the distance, behind a little wooden

shack, she could see where Roberto was trying to hide.
The mother ran over to where the little boy was hiding and
found that he had eaten all the figs except two which he
still held in his hand. She took him and tied him to the fig
tree. Then she dug a big hole in the ground nearby. When
she was through digging, she took the little boy and threw
him in the hole. As she was covering the hole with dirt, the
little boy kept saying, "Little Mother, please don't bury me!
Please don't bury me!" But she did not listen and covered
the hole up.

Later, when the father came home, he asked his wife
where the children were. "Rebecca is out in the yard playing
and Roberto has gone over to stay with some little friends
for a few days," she answered.

They had supper, but the husband was very disappointed
that his wife had no treat for him that night. After they
finished their supper, they all went to bed.

A few days later, when Rebecca was playing in the backyard under the fig tree, she noticed some funny-looking grass.
It was red and very fine like hair. She started to pull the
funny-looking grass out of the ground when she heard, "Little
Sister of my life, do not pull my hair out. For it is here that
I am buried, because I ate the figs we picked from the fig
tree."

Rebecca could not believe what she had heard. Once
again she pulled the red grass and once again the little voice
from the ground cried out. When the little girl asked who
had buried him there under the fig tree, there was no answer.
Frightened, she went into the house and called her father.

When the father came out into the backyard, Rebecca
showed him the red grass. He started pulling it out, but he
also heard a little voice coming out of the ground. It said,
"Little Father of my life, do not pull my hair out. For it is
here that I am buried, because I ate the figs we picked
from the fig tree."

Greatly puzzled, the father immediately asked who had buried him there under the fig tree. When there was no answer, he went into the house and brought out his wife. He showed her the red grass under the fig tree and told her to pull it. When she did pull the red grass, they all heard the voice from the ground say, "Little Mother of my life, do not pull my hair out. For it is here that you yourself buried me, because I ate the figs we picked from the fig tree."

The Tripe

This was a little boy whose mother sent him to the meat market for some *tripas*. She gave him the money with which to buy them, and she told him not to delay, because she wanted to fry them for supper.

The little boy started for the market, but before he got to the market, he came to a candy store. He bought candy with all the money his mother had given him.

After he had eaten all the candy he had bought, he remembered what he should have gotten. But now he did not have any money to buy the *tripas*. He was very much afraid of going home without them.

The little boy started walking around without too much direction. As he was walking along, he passed by a cemetery, and he saw a coffin beside an open grave. The little boy walked up closer to the coffin and saw that there was a corpse in it. He pulled out his pocketknife and cut the dead man's stomach open. He took out the corpse's *tripas*. Then he found a piece of paper like the kind used at the meat market for wrapping meat. He wrapped up the *tripas* so his mother would not suspect anything.

That evening, after he had taken the *tripas* to his mother and she had prepared them, they all sat down to eat supper. The little boy was not too hungry, for he knew what they were actually having for supper. His mother was puzzled when he would not eat. He did not know what to say, but finally he said he was not hungry, because he had eaten the *pilón* given him at the market. His mother was not convinced, and to keep her from asking further questions he ate some of the *tripas*.

Late that night, very close to midnight, when everyone in the neighborhood was asleep, the little boy began to hear strange noises. It sounded like a scratching or a digging noise. Then it sounded as if someone were pulling himself out of a grave. It was the corpse. He was digging himself out of his grave. The little boy started hearing footsteps. The sound of the footsteps was very faint at first. He could hardly hear them. Then the sound grew louder and louder and louder. It was as if the corpse was approaching the boy's house.

The heavy sound of footsteps followed by a dragging sound was now very clear to the boy. But he also started hearing, "I want my *tripas!* I want my *tripas!* I want my *tripas!*" The voice was very deep and tired-sounding. It was barely audible at first, but grew louder, rougher, and more demanding as it approached the house. The little boy was terrified when he heard the corpse say, "I am now out of my grave. I want my *tripas!* Give me back my *tripas.* I am now at the gate to the cemetery. I am now crossing the street. I am getting closer and closer to your house. I want my *tripas!*"

Then the little boy heard, "I am bloody and rotting. My eyes and hands are very ugly. Give me back my *tripas!* You can see my bones. My stomach is out and bloody. I want my *tripas!* I want my *tripas!*"

Finally the little boy heard the front door to his house open. The corpse informed him slowly of his approach up the stairway. He related his climb up the steps slowly and in a monotonous voice. Then he said, "I am getting to your bedroom door. I am beginning to open it—I am here! My *tripas!* My *tripas!* My *tripas!*" [With this ending, the teller makes a sudden grabbing motion for the listener's stomach.]

Contributors

FRANCIS E. ABERNETHY teaches English at Lamar State College of Technology in Beaumont.

ROGER ABRAHAMS is instructor in English at the University of Texas. He received the Ph.D. at the University of Pennsylvania, where he wrote, under the direction of MacEdward Leach, a dissertation on Negro folklore collected in Philadelphia.

RILEY AIKEN for many years taught modern languages at Kansas State College, Emporia. His contributions to the Texas Folklore Society Publications began in 1937 with his notable "A Pack Load of Mexican Tales." He has recently retired and now lives in Norman, Oklahoma.

JOHN Q. ANDERSON, a regular contributor to the annual publications of the Texas Folklore Society, is a professor of English at Texas A. and M. College.

A. L. BENNETT, who received the Ph.D. at the University of Texas, is professor of English at Texas A. and M. College.

MODY C. BOATRIGHT teaches English at the University of Texas.

ELIZABETH BRANDON is professor of French at the University of Houston. She is currently vice-president of the Texas Folklore Society.

LOIS BROCK wrote her paper on Tarantula Lore while a student at North Texas State University, from which she was graduated in 1960. She now teaches English in the Denver City (Texas) High School.

THEODORE B. BRUNNER was graduated from the University of Texas with a major in psychology. He collected his stories while taking Américo Paredes' course in the folktale. He is now teaching at Ohio State University.

ROSALINDA GONZALEZ wrote "Work and Play on a Border Ranch" while a student in Pan American College; her essay won third place in the Texas Folklore Society's college contest in 1959.

BALDEMAR A. JIMÉNEZ wrote "Cuentos de Susto" when he was a student of Américo Paredes' at the University of Texas.

JOHN C. MYERS is a teacher and counselor in the Eagle Pass public schools.

PAUL PATTERSON was growing up in the cow pastures of Gaines, Reagan, and Upton counties before the landscape was ruined by oil derricks and when horsepower was largely in the horse. He is a graduate of Sul Ross State College and a teacher of Spanish and journalism at Crane.

RICHARD M. RIVERS collected his stories while studying the folktale under Américo Paredes at the University of Texas. He is now in business in Abilene.

Index